D0867436

"As we have come to expect from Professor d carefully written, thoughtfully examined, and graciously interpreted study of the book of Hebrews. Readers who seek to become more faithful disciples of Jesus through a study of Scripture will find no better guide."
—**Emerson B. Powery**, Professor of Biblical Studies, Messiah College

"Hebrews, as David deSilva rightly reminds us, is a very eloquent, Scripture-rich sermon. Not a letter, not a Gospel, not an Acts, not an apocalypse, but a sermon—one meant to ward off defections due to attempts at shaming the converts being addressed. This helpful study places us all in the original setting of the letter and lets us hear once more the real force and fervor, the real thrust and theology of the original sermon. This is an ideal study for those looking to understand this too often neglected NT document better. Highly recommended."
—**Ben Witherington, III**, Amos Professor of New Testament for Doctoral Studies, Asbury Theological Seminary

"In this work, brilliant New Testament scholar David deSilva opens up the book of Hebrews in an expert and readable manner. This is an excellent resource to get the basic background and message of the book and its constituent argument and passages."
—**Craig S. Keener**, F. M. and Ada Thompson Professor of Biblical Studies, Asbury Theological Seminary

"The Letter to the Hebrews is a rich and powerful work, but it can also be quite difficult for modern readers to understand. In this study, David deSilva walks us through Hebrews with both scholarly expertise and pastoral sensitivity. The result is a powerful engagement with Hebrews that will draw readers into the Scriptures and closer to God. Highly recommended!"
—**David F. Watson**, Academic Dean, United Theological Seminary

"David deSilva is a brilliant New Testament scholar who writes in service to the church. In his commentary on Hebrews, he connects the radical gift of our great high priest, Jesus Christ, with the gracious response of a life offered in response to God's giving. This reflection on scripture will ground disciples in the daily call to become more like Jesus."
—**Kenneth H. Carter**, Bishop, Florida Conference, The United Methodist Church

Selected Books by David A. deSilva

Breaking the Code, Revised Edition
(Bruce M. Metzger, revisions by David A. deSilva)

The Apocrypha
(Core Biblical Studies)

Invitation to the New Testament
(Disciple Bible Study; with Emerson Powery)

Paul and the Macedonians
(Life and Letters of Paul)

Transformation: The Heart of Paul's Gospel
(Lexham)

Sacramental Life
(InterVarsity)

Praying with John Wesley
(Discipleship Resources)

New Testament Themes
(Chalice)

Honor, Patronage, Kinship & Purity
(InterVarsity)

Day of Atonement: A Novel of the Maccabean Revolt
(Kregel)

DAVID A. deSILVA

HEBREWS

GRACE AND GRATITUDE

Abingdon Press / Nashville

HEBREWS
GRACE AND GRATITUDE

Copyright © 2020 Abingdon Press
All rights reserved.

Library of Congress Control Number: 2020932523
ISBN 13: 978-1-5018-9610-1

20 21 22 23 24 25 26 27 28 29—10 9 8 7 6 5 4 3 2 1
MANUFACTURED IN THE UNITED STATES OF AMERICA

To my parents,
J. Arthur and Dorothy A. de Silva,
in honor of their sixtieth wedding anniversary

and

to my wife,
Donna Jean,
in honor of our thirtieth

Contents

Introduction

Following Jesus means committing yourself to him completely. Does Jesus really offer you enough to make it worth investing that much—your whole life? Do you find yourself pulling back from serving Christ and bearing witness to Christ as fully as you feel called because you're concerned that your neighbors and associates might start viewing you less favorably? Do you tend to give God what is left over from your time and energy after giving the lion's share to everything else? Do you ever wonder if perhaps God desires and deserves *more* from you, given what God has done and promises to do for you according to our faith?

These are not new questions or problems. Our sisters and brothers in the first-century house churches faced them all and struggled just as we do with staying the course they began when they first put their trust in Jesus. The early Christian teacher who wrote our "Letter to the Hebrews" confronts these questions head-on with one of the most theologically rich reflections on the person and work of Jesus that we find in the New Testament—and one of the most robust pictures of what faithful discipleship, lived in response to this Jesus, looks like in action. In Hebrews, we find a source of encouragement to follow Jesus wholeheartedly and with our full lives, grateful for all that God has provided and trusting in all that he promises.

"We have . . ."

"*We have . . .*" Over the course of his brief exhortation, the author of Hebrews finishes this sentence in many ways. We have "a great high priest who has crossed through the heavens" (4:14; 8:1). We have "strong confidence to grasp the hope that lies before us" (6:18).

We have "a firm and secure anchor for the soul" (6:19). We have "boldness to enter the holy places by the blood of Jesus" (10:19). We have "better and lasting possessions" (10:34). We have "a great cloud of witnesses surrounding us" (12:1). We have "an altar from which [others] have no authority to eat" (13:10). The writer reminds his readers of all they have received through Christ.

The Christians he addressed had lost a great deal since they came to faith in Jesus and began bringing their lives in line with their convictions. The Gentiles among them resolved not to worship any god but the One, which made them appear antisocial, as the worship of the traditional Greco-Roman gods pervaded social, civic, and economic life in their cities. The Jews among them began eating with Gentiles as with sisters and brothers, allowing the Holy Spirit and the teachings of Jesus (a crucified blasphemer!), and not the ancestral Jewish law, to regulate their lives. The Christian audience of Hebrews found themselves treated as deviants. Their non-Christian neighbors, both Gentiles and Jews, regarded them as traitors to the way of life into which they had been born. The non-Christians openly humiliated Christians. They robbed and impoverished some of them. They even physically assaulted some Christians and had some thrown into prison on trumped-up charges (10:32-34). Their goal was to convince the followers of Jesus that their new way of life was not worth the cost. The Christians had remained firm in their faith and helped keep one another on track for some time, but their neighbors' constant antagonism was beginning to achieve its goal, as some Christians had already stopped openly associating themselves with the group altogether (10:25).

From beginning to end, the author of Hebrews sought to remind these believers of how much they had *gained* as a result of coming to faith and living faithfully. True, their commitment had not been without cost. But this cost paled in comparison with what they had acquired and were yet to acquire (if God's promises were to be trusted). It also paled in comparison with the cost that Jesus, the Son of God, their deliverer, willingly paid in order to bring them these great benefits. And in Jesus they had access to all the resources they needed to press on until they arrived at the everlasting homeland that God had prepared for them.

"Because we have. . ."

The author was not, however, simply keen on reminding his audience of the benefits they had received from God through Jesus or of the greater gifts yet to come, as if taking inventory. He reminded them from beginning to end that great gifts call for great gratitude, that every act of giving calls forth acts in response. This conviction pulses throughout the Book of Hebrews, even as it pulsed through the daily lives of the author, the Christian audience, and even their non-Christian neighbors. They would all have known that a gift was not merely about the transfer of a commodity from one person to another. It was an act that initiated a relationship, a virtuous action that prompted—and necessitated—a virtuous reaction.

And so the author writes not simply "we *have*," but "*because* we have":

> Because we have a great high priest who has crossed through the heavens—Jesus, the Son of God—let us hold onto our testimony! . . . Let us keep drawing closer to the throne of favor with boldness, so that we may receive mercy and find favor for timely help! (4:14, 16)

> Because we have boldness to enter the holy places by Jesus's blood . . . and a great high priest over God's house, let us keep drawing closer. . . . Let us hold onto our profession of hope without wavering. . . . Let us consider one another closely with the result that we will break forth in love and good works, not neglecting to come together (as is the habit of some) but encouraging one another.
>
> (10:19-25)

> Because we are receiving an unshakable kingdom, let us
> show gratitude! (12:28)

The author wants his hearers' lives to continue to take shape not in response to their neighbors' *taking away*, but in response to God's *giving*. He dwells on the magnitude of God's gifts and of the place of unprecedented favor in which followers of Christ stand in order to magnify the importance of responding gratefully to such a Giver. He dwells on the Son's complete commitment to and investment in *them* in order to call forth a commitment and investment from them to match.

The focal point of this study of the "Letter to the Hebrews" will be these themes of grace and response that dominate this early Christian sermon—the gifts offered to us in Christ and the gratitude that such generosity rightly evokes. This message is vitally important for Christians throughout parts of Africa, the Middle East, and South Asia, who can readily identify with the situation of the original audience since they face the same pressures (and worse) in the present time. Such believers must constantly shore up their conviction that God's favor and benefits are worth the cost of keeping faith with God, no matter what pressures are brought to bear on them to mute their witness and compromise their obedience to God. But this message is equally important for Christians in the United States and other settings in which our faith arouses considerably less hostility—and often not even any interest—among our neighbors. You and I are no less at risk of being swept along in the current of our society's agendas and practices rather than holding fast to the anchor of our hope and living against the cultural stream into God's vision for our lives.

The author of Hebrews gives forceful expression to the gospel's claim upon our whole selves. If we respond to this claim as the preacher hoped his original audience would respond, our lives will reflect a greater integrity. Our convictions will shape our direction.

Our affirmations of faith will shape our aspirations for life. Our daily practices will align with those of the people of faith who constitute that "great cloud of witnesses" celebrated in 11:1–12:3, and we will give consistent evidence to the people around us of the certainty of God's gifts and promises, because their *effects* are clearly seen in how we use *our* lives in response.

If there is a prayer in the Christian tradition that captures the pulse of our author's desire for his own congregation, it is "The General Thanksgiving" that closes the orders for morning and evening prayer in *The Book of Common Prayer.* After rehearsing the many ways in which God graciously intervenes in our lives, from our creation to our daily sustenance to God's "redemption of the world by our Lord Jesus Christ," the prayer concludes:

> Give us such an awareness of your mercies,
> that with truly thankful hearts we may show forth your praise,
> not only with our lips, but in our lives,
> by giving up our selves to your service,
> and by walking before you
> in holiness and righteousness all our days;
> through Jesus Christ our Lord.[1]

One

The Sermon's Setting and the Son's Glory

(Hebrews 1:1–2:4)

Do we think enough of Jesus? The question can have two senses, and both are important. The first sense is this: Do we hold him in high enough regard? Do we sufficiently appreciate Jesus's stature in God's sight and his achievements on our behalf? And the second sense is: Do we think of Jesus enough? Do we give our attention sufficiently to Jesus, his work, and his worth—that is, the respect and service he merits from us—throughout each day? Or do we think of him too infrequently as we give our attention to so many other matters from so many other angles?

The preacher who composed the "Letter to the Hebrews" understood that failing to think enough of Jesus—in both senses— would eventually undermine our commitment to discipleship. As other concerns rise in both importance and frequency above our concern to follow, honor, and obey Jesus, we drift off track from the direction God calls us and settle back all too easily into the ruts of the life from which he seeks to save us. If we think too little of Jesus, our lives will fail to reflect what they ought most to reflect—our gratitude to our Redeemer and Advocate, our devotion to him who devoted his all to us.

The author of Hebrews therefore begins his sermon by drawing our attention to Jesus afresh. From the opening sentence he invites us to consider Jesus's place in God's cosmic scheme beyond the confines of "the days of his flesh," so to speak, to fathom the honor that is his by right as Son of God, and to feel the pull of his gravity upon our attention and lives. In this way, the preacher positions his hearers in every place and time to give the highest priority to the deliverance that Jesus has secured for us and to walking in the way that reflects our esteem for him and his gifts. For it is in our daily choices and practices that we show Jesus and the world around us precisely how much or how little we think of him.

The Preacher and His Congregation

The starting point for discovering what scripture says to us is training ourselves to listen to what scripture said "to them," that is, to the people for whom that scriptural text was originally written. Only after we have listened for scripture's *timely* message for those people for whom it was written can we reliably hear scripture's *timeless* message (or, better, its new timely message) for us.

This is especially true for the books from Romans through Revelation, all of which were written with specific goals in mind, for a specific audience facing specific circumstances. The typical opening of these books often provides us with important information about the audience and their situation that helps us understand that timely message. For example, 1 Corinthians begins with the words: "Paul, commissioned an apostle of Jesus Christ by God's will, and our brother Sosthenes, to God's assembly in Corinth" (1 Corinthians 1:1-2). This tells us who is writing and to whom, and it happens that we have access to a great deal of information about this congregation and its setting both from the archaeological record and from Acts of the Apostles, which recounts the story of Paul's initial visit and work in Corinth. Or, for another example, consider James 1:1: "James, a slave of God and of the Lord Jesus Christ, to the twelve tribes in the Dispersion, greetings." As a starting point, we might read the letter as written by James, the head of the Jerusalem Church, particularly with a view to addressing Jewish Christians (the primary sphere of James's authority and interest) throughout the Roman empire.

Notice, however, that the Book of Hebrews does *not* begin in this way. We do not read in Hebrews 1:1 that Paul or James or any other person wrote to a community known as the Hebrews (Christian or otherwise). Instead, the author launches right into the message: "In the past, God spoke through the prophets" (1:1). Our text identifies neither the writer nor the recipients.

The author's identity was a matter of debate even in the early church. The one sure fact was that the author knew Timothy, long-time partner of Paul, with whose travel plans he seeks to coordinate his own (13:23). This puts the author firmly in the circle of Paul's team, but this was a large pool of Christian workers. Early church fathers pointed to Barnabas or Apollos (known for his eloquence, as reflected in Acts 18:24) as possible authors, alongside Paul. Over time there was an increasing tendency to attribute the book to Paul, which went hand-in-hand with the church's desire to affirm its scriptural authority. Apostolic authorship would have strengthened its case.

Paul seems to me the least likely candidate to have written Hebrews, however, since the author admits to coming to faith through the testimony of Jesus's witnesses (Hebrews 2:2-4), whereas Paul is adamant that he came to faith through a direct encounter with the glorified Christ and emphatically *not* through human messengers (Galatians 1:1, 11-17; 1 Corinthians 15:3-10). Paul also claims to have avoided trying to achieve persuasion through high-sounding rhetoric because he wanted conviction to come through the Holy Spirit (1 Corinthians 2:1-5). High-sounding rhetoric, however, is precisely what the author of Hebrews prefers.

Second-century scribes would give the text a title similar to other titles like "To the Romans" and "To the Galatians" based on their conjecture that Paul or someone connected to his mission had written it to a specific Christian community. Because of the author's intense interest in the story of the Hebrews in the desert (3:7–4:13) and the desert tabernacle and its sacrificial rites (7:1–10:18), scribes began to name it "To the Hebrews." Modern readers tend to accept this conjecture on the basis of their own prejudice: Who but Jews or Jewish Christians would be as interested or well versed in the Old Testament as the author presumes his audience to be?[1] We tend to forget, however, that what we call the "Old Testament" was the *only* Testament for the earliest churches and that the message about Jesus as the Messiah was thoroughly grounded in that Testament for both Jews and non-Jews drawn to the Christian movement. Gentile converts would become thoroughly familiar with its contents and deeply interested to understand how they themselves related to the historic people of God who were constantly in focus in those scriptures.

The conjecture becomes even more questionable when we consider the very essence of Paul's mission, with which this author was connected. Paul understood his calling to be to proclaim the Messiah of Israel as the Savior of the Gentiles, calling non-Jews away from the worship of their idols to the worship of the One God, the God of Jew and Gentile alike. He might well have nurtured *mixed* communities of Christians from both Jewish and non-Jewish backgrounds—as appears to have been the case in Syrian Antioch (see Galatians 2:11-14)—but any text addressed to a congregation born of Paul's mission would have addressed Gentile converts at least as much as Jewish converts.

The beginning of Hebrews does not identify its writer or its audience, but it does show us something of the writer's skill. Hebrews begins with one of the most artfully crafted and rhetorically balanced sentences in the New Testament:

> In the past, God spoke through the prophets to our ancestors in many times and many ways. In these final days, though, he spoke to us through a Son. God made his Son the heir of everything and created the world through him.

> The Son is the light of God's glory and the imprint of God's being. He maintains everything with his powerful message. After he carried out the cleansing of people from their sins, he sat down at the right side of the highest majesty. And the Son became so much greater than the other messengers, such as angels, that he received a more important title than theirs. (1:1-4 CEB)

These first four verses of Hebrews are a single sentence in Greek, which is full of internal rhymes and matching cadences. The opening line uses the still-familiar preacher's trick called alliteration, the use of a single sound to begin multiple words. If we were to try to capture this in English, we might write: "Piecemeal and partial were God's past pronouncements to the patriarchs through the prophets." The person who listens to this opening would not think of it as a "letter" at all, but as a sermon. Indeed, this is how the author himself classifies his text when he calls it a "word of exhortation" (13:22), a term used elsewhere for a sermon or homily (as in Acts 13:15). Hebrews, these clues suggest, is most likely an early Christian sermon.

William Lane has described this text as "a sermon in search of a setting."[2] There is one clue concerning the location of either the preacher or the congregation. In the closing remarks the preacher adds: "The group from Italy greets you" (Hebrews 13:24 CEB). This strongly suggests *some* connection with Christianity in Italy (most likely in Rome), but it is not clear whether Christians in Italy were sending their greetings to the audience in some other place, or whether expatriate Italian Christians were sending their greetings to the congregation "back home." The sermon had to have been composed before AD 96, when Clement of Rome quoted it in his letter to the Christians in Corinth. References to the sacrifices prescribed by the Jewish law as ongoing further suggest a date prior to AD 70 and the temple's destruction—when, in fact, they did "cease to be offered" (Hebrews 10:1-2).

Despite these unknowns, the author does throw open some clear windows on the story and the setting of his audience. He reminded them of their experience of coming to faith in response to the apostolic preaching—an experience that the author believed to have included unmistakable signs of God "showing up" to confirm the truth of the gospel message (2:1-4).[3] He recalled their thorough grounding in the fundamentals of the faith, including their turning away from a dead-end life toward the living God, their life-changing experiences of baptism and receiving the Holy Spirit, and their awareness of accountability to God and life beyond death (6:1-3). As mentioned above, the Christians' neighbors reacted to their new commitments and practices with hostile rejection, using all the means at their disposal to dissuade them from continuing in their new path. Nevertheless, the believers had bravely endured in the face of a wide variety of pressures. Even those who had not been specifically targeted by their neighbors had put themselves in harm's way in order to encourage and show solidarity with their Christian family (10:32-34).

But those were "the earlier days" (10:32). Things had begun to change by the time the author addressed them with this sermon— and these changes were what *prompted* him to address them. These Christians had suffered the loss of a secure place and honorable status in this world without seeing the fulfillment of God's promises of a better place and status. It had been growing increasingly difficult for some to live in that in-between space of no longer being at home here but not yet finding a home there in some "kingdom of God." Some Christians had begun to pull back from associating with the group, starting their journey back toward their neighbors' approval, trading in their witness to Christ's benefits for the chance to regain some stability in this life (10:25). The author wrote to stave off any more such "drifting away" (2:1). In the author's mind, this was not some harmless change of heart. It was a grave insult that amounts to "turn[ing] away from the living God" (3:12) and "trampling God's Son underfoot" (10:29). It is a decision to exchange God's favor for God's wrath (6:4-8; 10:29-31). The author is also concerned that the other Christians did not invest themselves sufficiently in their sisters and brothers to prevent their defection (5:11-14).

The author composed his sermon, therefore, in order to achieve particular effects in his audience in light of these specific challenges:

- He sought, above all, to magnify the present and eternal advantages they possess as a result of their connection with Jesus—the Son of God!—so as to keep them from deciding that the temporary disadvantages of this connection outweigh the advantages.

- He magnified the disadvantages of valuing God's favor and the Son's investment in them too lightly, urging his audience to think first and foremost about the honor, loyalty, and service due God and God's Messiah in response.

- He insulated them against the effects of the shaming they are experiencing by showing, first, that people of faith have typically had to ignore or despise shame (above all, Jesus himself, 12:2!) and, second, by turning their endurance of harassment into an opportunity to win honor in God's sight.

- He mobilized the Christian community to look out for and shore up the commitment of the wavering, so that each believer's experience of love and support within the congregation outpaced the discouragement and pressures from outside.

The author braids these four threads into a strong cord by which to tether his sisters and brothers to the hope that anchors them in their eternal inheritance even in the midst of the storms that assail them on this side of reaching that harbor.

God's Ultimate Messenger

Etched into the pulpit in the Ashland Theological Seminary chapel is a reminder to every preacher who stands in that space: "Always give them Jesus." This is precisely how the author of Hebrews began his sermon. Given what his audience had been experiencing, he could have started elsewhere. He could have begun by acknowledging his audience's circumstances: "I know a lot of you have suffered a great deal and given up a lot over the past few years." He could have begun by drawing attention to their failings: "I've heard that some of your people have stopped coming out to worship and that the rest of you haven't done a thing about it!" Instead, he begins by drawing his hearers' attention to Jesus. He begins with a forceful declaration about how God has spoken to them in a Son. The God who had given shadowy hints and pointers concerning God's plans through the prophets has now given a definitive revelation of God's purposes and promises through God's own Son.

The preacher positions his congregation to reevaluate what is truly important in their history, that is, which events in their history should drive their present and future. The most important thing is not, he suggests, that they're having a tough time of things because their neighbors are unhappy with them and putting pressure on them. It's that God, the almighty ruler of the cosmos, has spoken a definitive word about deliverance through God's own Son, God's partner in creation, God's agent in sustaining the cosmic order, a being who bears the very imprint and image of God, who took on flesh for a brief span in order to accomplish something vitally important at great personal cost, and then returned to the divine realm to take his seat at the right hand of the Majesty in heaven! Now *that's* an incredible event in recent history, worthy of their continued, *full* attention. Whatever negative messages they were hearing from their neighbors—and even from within as they listened to their own doubts and apprehensions—they had to remember that God had spoken and that heeding God's message must always take top priority.

In the course of driving this point home, the preacher has a great deal to say about who Jesus is and what Jesus has achieved on our behalf. Indeed, he opens his sermon with one of the loftiest statements about Jesus's person and significance in the whole New Testament. Let's look again at the opening words:

> The God who spoke to our ancestors through the prophets in varied and piecemeal fashion has, in these most recent days, spoken to us in a Son whom he appointed to be the heir of all things, through whom he also made the ages— who, being the radiance of God's glory and the imprint of God's very essence, sustaining all things by his powerful word, having himself made purification for sins, sat down at the right hand of the Majesty in the high places, having become so much greater than the angels as the name he has inherited is more distinguished than theirs. (1:1-4)

For the preacher, Jesus's story does not start with his birth to Mary and Joseph. As God's Son, his story reaches back to before the beginning.

The language that the preacher uses to talk about the Son's relationship to God—"the radiance of God's glory and the imprint of God's very essence"—recalls language that other Jewish authors used to speak about the relationship of Wisdom to God. For example, the author of Wisdom of Solomon writes: "she [Wisdom] is the reflection of eternal light . . . and the image of God's goodness" (Wisdom of Solomon 7:26). Jewish sages spoke of the personified figure of Wisdom as God's companion and partner in the creation of the world and as God's agent in sustaining it (Proverbs 8:27-31; Wisdom of Solomon 7:22, 27; 9:9). As far as the author of Hebrews was concerned, when the Word became flesh, Wisdom was shown to have a definitive face—the face of God's Son, Jesus. With the author of the Gospel of John, he shares the conviction that to see the Son is to see the Father (compare John 1:18; 14:8-9). In Jesus's compassion and selfless love, we see *God's* compassion and selfless love. In Jesus's desire to extend healing and hope to people of all walks of life, we see *God's* desire to bring all people to know God's love and fellowship. In Jesus's giving himself over to a brutal death to make "purification for sins," we see God's yearning to forgive and restore us to favor.

According to the preacher, God brought the world into being through the Son, governs the world through the Son, and will bring the world to its consummation through the Son. What, then, could be more important and more urgent than how we continue to respond to this Son? The author will bring his hearers back to this point repeatedly throughout his sermon (Hebrews 2:1-4; 3:7-8, 14-15; 12:25-29).

The Son, the Scriptures, and the Angels

The preacher gives a sampling of how he understands God's earlier pronouncements through the prophets (who, for the preacher, include the authors of the psalms) as he continues the opening of his sermon (1:5-14). His practice is often to consider the meaning of an Old Testament passage when read as if spoken *about* the Son, *to* the Son, or even *by* the Son. We might wonder whether the preacher is playing fast and loose with the Old Testament Scriptures (a charge frequently thrown around in discussions of the interpretation of the Old Testament in the New). Did the prophets really talk about Jesus in their original context? Or were they speaking about someone or something else entirely?

The writer of Hebrews, however, actually shows a high degree of sophistication in his selection of scriptures in this opening chapter. Most of the passages he recites in verses 5-14 come from the "royal psalms"[4] that were composed with the Davidic king as their subject or related texts, such as 2 Samuel 7:14. When Zedekiah, king of Judah, was removed from power and deported in disgrace to Babylon in 587 BC, David's line came to end. The royal psalms began, then, to be read as expressions of hope for the restoration of this line, for the coming of the Messiah, the "anointed" heir of David's kingdom. In light of the preacher's conviction that Jesus (a man of David's line;

see Matthew 1:1, 6, 17; Luke 1:27, 32-33; Romans 1:3) was this Anointed One, reading the royal psalms as addressing Jesus, the Son, was entirely appropriate.

The main theme that this flurry of scriptural quotations supports was announced at the close of the sermon's first (long) sentence: as God's Son, Jesus possesses a significantly greater dignity than even the angels of God (1:4). God had never addressed one of his angels as God's "Son," but this is how the heir of the kingdom was addressed both in a royal psalm (Psalm 2:7) and in God's promise to David (2 Samuel 7:14) referenced in Hebrews 1:5:

> For to which one of the angels did God ever say, "You are my Son; today have I begotten you," and again, "I myself will be a father to him, and he himself will be a son to me"?

The preacher and his congregation might well be familiar with stories about Jesus's baptism (Mark 1:11) or transfiguration (Mark 9:7), in which God was remembered to have addressed him directly as "Son" in alignment with these earlier promises. They would certainly have been familiar with Paul's proclamation of Jesus as God's "Son" as in Galatians 1:16; 2:20; 4:4; and 1 Thessalonians 1:10.

The preacher moves next to a verse in the Song of Moses in Deuteronomy 32. In the midst of a paragraph celebrating the certainty of God's future interventions to vindicate God's people and subdue God's enemies, the preacher's version of Deuteronomy reads, "let all God's angels fall down before him" (Hebrews 1:6). The preacher takes the surprising step here of applying this invitation specifically to God's recalling the Son to the unshakable "world" of the eternal realm—surprising, because the Song of Moses was not typically read as a messianic text.[5] Here it becomes, however, another scriptural witness to the Son's elevation above the angels, who are now to show the Son the same honor that they show God.

The preacher then returns to additional royal psalms to speak further of the Son's elevation above his (heavenly) colleagues:

> Of the angels he says, "The one making winds his messen-
> gers and fiery flames his servants." But of the Son he says,
> "Your throne, O God, is forever, and your kingly scepter
> is a scepter of righteousness. You have loved justice and
> hated lawlessness: for this reason God, your God, anointed
> you above your peers with the oil of gladness."
> (Hebrews 1:7-9, quoting Psalm 104:4 and 45:6-7)

Compared with the Son, whose rule is grounded in the eternal rule
of God, angelic beings, however glorious and powerful they might be
imagined to be, are mere functionaries.

The thought of the permanence of God's rule leads the author to
take a step further in this direction with his next breath, comparing
the Son now not with the angels but with creation itself:

> And, "You laid the foundations of the earth from the
> beginning, Lord, and the heavens are the works of your
> hands: these will perish, but you will persist. All will wear
> out like a garment, and like a scroll you will roll them up;
> like a garment they will be changed out. But you remain
> the same and your years will never run out!"
> (Hebrews 1:10-12, quoting Psalm 102:25-27)

The preacher hints here at a major theme that will run throughout
his sermon. The things of this world, of this creation, will not last. The
material world that seems so real to us who believe in what we can see
and touch and quantify is destined to "wear out like an old garment,"
indeed to be dramatically shaken off its hinges and removed so that the
way into God's eternal realm may one day become apparent (Hebrews
12:26-28). God and God's Son, however, existed before this material
creation and will exist far beyond it. How could it ever be a good
investment, therefore, to acquire a larger share of what is temporary
at the cost of relinquishing a share of what is eternal—or of alienating
the one who is eternal? This is a question that the preacher will bring
before his congregation again and again before he ends his sermon.

When the preacher says of the Son, "you remain the same," he is tapping into a topic of dependability and trust. He will return even more forcefully to this at the conclusion of his sermon when he declares, "Jesus Christ—yesterday and today the same, and always!" (13:8). Dio Chrysostom, a Greek orator active in the late first and early second centuries AD, complained that is was difficult to trust people because "no one knows about any one whether he or she will remain the same until tomorrow. . . . With human beings there is no constancy or truthfulness at all."[6] A person might make promises today but not fulfill them tomorrow, not because "things change" (a frequently heard excuse!), but because *people* change and prove untrustworthy. The Son of God is not like that, the preacher affirms. We can hold onto the same trust that our own teachers in the faith, and their teachers, and *their* teachers put in Jesus because Jesus will be "tomorrow" as we found him to be "yesterday and today" (Hebrews 13:7-8).

The preacher was justifiably suspicious of all that belongs to the life of this world. We, too, can readily recognize the fickleness and unpredictability of the world we inhabit. The economy fluctuates wildly, leaving investors elated today and alarmed tomorrow. Terrorists continue to remind people in many countries just how vulnerable we all are. Disease and accidents regularly testify to the fragility of our lives. "Here we have no enduring city," the preacher will say near the end of his sermon (13:14). Rather, we have been given the promise of a "city that has foundations," which cannot be shaken by the changes and chances of this life, "whose architect and builder is God" (11:10). He will challenge his congregation to walk in line with and toward that hope. He emboldens them to allow their lives in this world to continue to crumble around them, knowing that this world itself is destined for crumbling as a whole. If they want to hold onto what will endure—their "better and lasting possessions" (10:34), their "better, heavenly homeland" (11:16), their "lasting city" (13:14)—they have to hold onto Jesus, who will ultimately prove to be their security, their sure foundation, their anchor that moors them even now in their eternal harbor.

The preacher returns to the subject of the angels again in 1:13-14, quoting a verse from another royal psalm that will become a touchstone for the whole sermon:

> And to which of the angels has he ever said, "Sit at my right hand until I place your enemies as a footstool under your feet"? (Hebrews 1:13, quoting Psalm 110:1)[7]

The form of the quotation recalls the verse that launched us into this chain of scriptures (Hebrews 1:5), asking when such wonderful things said to the Son were ever said to an angel. The preacher's choice of Old Testament texts resonates once again with stories about Jesus. In Mark, after successfully answering or deflecting a series of challenges from rival Jewish leaders, Jesus posed a challenge of his own:

> Responding to [the scribes], Jesus was saying while teaching in the temple: "How can the scribes say that the Messiah is David's son? David himself says in the Holy Spirit, 'The Lord said to my Lord, "Sit at my right hand until I place your enemies beneath your feet".' David himself calls him 'Lord', so how is he his son?" (Mark 12:35-37)

Early Christians read this verse in connection with Jesus's ascension forty days after his resurrection from the dead. It became the (unspoken) divine invitation to which the ascension was the response and the verse that interpreted the ascension as God's exaltation of Jesus to the place of highest honor in the cosmos, appointing Jesus God's "right-hand person."

The preacher draws his comparison to a close with a statement about the angels in the form of a rhetorical question (rhetorical, because the audience can answer *only* yes at this point): "Aren't they all ministering spirits sent out for service on behalf of those who are about to inherit salvation?" (Hebrews 1:14). If we read closely, we might be surprised that this preacher describes Christian disciples not as people who have already been "saved," but as people who are "*about* to inherit salvation." He is deeply aware that he and his congregation have only *begun* their journey toward salvation—toward deliverance—when they believed the message about Jesus and placed their trust in him. This was both a deliverance *from* and deliverance *for*. It is a deliverance from the dissolution of the present creation, from God's judgment upon those who failed to honor their Creator with gratitude and obedience, and from the power of death itself. It is a deliverance for unending life in God's very presence. "Salvation" is what they would enjoy fully only when Christ came "a second time" (9:28), shaking the earth and heavens so as to open the way into their unshakable kingdom (12:26-28). The preacher did not speak this way to make his congregation insecure about their salvation. No one could take it away from them. He spoke this way to secure their commitment to persevere to the end of the journey, lest they throw away the deliverance that Jesus had won for them.[8] It was a journey in which they had to continue to press forward (6:1), persevering in a faithful and obedient response, until they were finally and firmly in their eternal city.

Fighting the Drift

Why does the preacher spend ten verses lining out scriptural support for his claim that the Son's dignity far outstrips that of the angels? Were the members of the congregation being drawn away from the worship of Jesus toward the worship of angels, as some scholars have suggested? Probably not. Indeed, the way the author uses rhetorical questions both at the opening and closing of this block (1:5, 13) suggests that his audience would have been in essential agreement with him all along the way. And when the preacher gets to the "so what" of his opening chapter, he says nothing about the practice of worshipping angels as the problem to be addressed.

Rather, he stresses the fact that the Son's honor exceeds that of the angels in order to drive home a very different point: neglecting the Son's message now would be far more dangerous than neglecting the angels' message:

> Because of this, it is imperative that we continue to pay close attention to what we have heard, lest we start drifting away. For if the message communicated through angels was firm and every transgression and disobedient act received due payback, how will we escape after showing disregard for so great a deliverance—one that, announced at first through the Lord, was confirmed to us by those who heard, with God testifying alongside them by means of signs and wonders and various manifestations of power and distributions of the Holy Spirit in line with God's will?
>
> (Hebrews 2:1-4)

What message was communicated through angels? Surprisingly, the preacher has in mind here the Law that was given to Moses on Mount Sinai. While not found in the accounts in Exodus or Deuteronomy, by the first century AD it had become commonplace to speak of angels having a role in bringing the Law from God to Moses (see, for example, Galatians 3:19; Acts 7:38, 53; and the nonbiblical Book of *Jubilees* 1:27-29; 2:1). This was probably a consequence of the expanding presence and role of angels (and demons!) generally in the thought and literature of Jews in the centuries before Christ. If the Law of Moses—the word brought through angels—was strictly enforced, such that those who violated the Law might even be put to death, the word that was brought through God's Son must surely command even greater attention and respect, even as the Son himself commands greater respect than the angels.

The preacher identifies the principal danger here as "drifting away" (2:1), the result of not giving the word *about* Jesus and the words *of* Jesus their due weight, of not remaining sufficiently mindful of their gravity such that they continue to exert the primary "pull" on the direction of our lives day by day. The believers who had stopped gathering with the worshipping community demonstrated this danger (10:25). What to them probably felt like getting their lives "back on track" the preacher regarded as "drifting off course." They were probably not thinking wrong things about Jesus, but they were certainly thinking *too little* of Jesus and of the deliverance and the salvation that he offered them. And this was a deliverance that would not be enjoyed merely by calling Jesus "Lord" at some point, but by living under his lordship through the thick and thin of daily life until they stood before their returning lord and greeted him as those who had lived faithfully for him.

Somewhat subtly in the opening of his sermon, the preacher introduces two options for that encounter with the returning Jesus. The Son, enthroned at God's right hand, looks ahead now to the subjection of his enemies (1:13); those who continued to heed the message God spoke through the Son could look ahead now to deliverance at the same time (1:14). But if, in this interim, the believers shrank back to align themselves with their neighbors—testifying to them by their very return to regular life that Jesus and his gifts were not worth the cost of keeping them—what kind of encounter with Jesus should they expect on the Day of the Lord? The preacher will return to these options throughout his sermon less and less subtly as he drives his congregation to consider carefully how they are positioning themselves to encounter the Son at his coming again (6:7-8; 10:19-31; 12:18-29).

The preacher warns us of the very real danger to our faith that arises when we give our first and best attention to getting ahead in the systems and economies of this world, to gathering up a larger share of this world's goods, or simply to enjoying this world's entertainments. When we only fit "religion" into our lives, rather than let the gospel of Christ shape the whole of our lives, we are not giving "due attention to what we have heard" (Hebrews 2:1), and we are underestimating the dignity of the Son who brought that message to us. The drift will show in our lives because we will be aiming for and investing our best efforts in attaining and maintaining a certain quality of life for ourselves and our own in the here and now. But our lives will take a very different direction if our first priorities are to live in line with Jesus's teachings and example, to attain and maintain a certain quality of life for *others* in the here and now, and to give ourselves over to letting God achieve God's purposes in the world through our willing agency. The preacher assures us, however, that moving in this direction leads toward deliverance on the day Christ returns by showing us to be loyal subjects of his kingdom.

Fighting the drift requires, of course, strong assurance about which course puts one's life on track. The preacher's audience had already made significant sacrifices in order to remain faithful to Jesus and to each other as long as they had. They needed assurance that they were making a good investment, that the reward would, in the end, justify the costs and the risks. They needed to know that they weren't just throwing away the only rewards of which human beings could be certain, like the enjoyment of quiet and peaceful lives, providing adequately for oneself and one's family, and having the respect and affirmation of one's neighbors.

The preacher reminds them of what they experienced as they began this journey, laying out the sources to which they might look back for that assurance. The word in which they had placed their hope, and in light of which they had reoriented their lives, was spoken by the incarnate Son and conveyed to them by those who had direct contact with him (Hebrews 2:3). The message of the gospel was not just a bundle of noble ideas and sentiments. It was rooted in the encounter with the power of God in the ministry, miracles, death, resurrection, and ascension of Jesus—events whose reality could be confirmed "by those who heard" and otherwise witnessed them (2:3). The resurrection of Jesus from the dead was a critically important event in this chain, for it meant God's own validation of Jesus's message about the life that pleased God. The congregation, however, had far more than the testimony of others as a basis for their assurance. They also had their own experience of God's presence and power in their midst. God showed up, as it were, to certify the truth of the message they had heard in ways that unmistakably bore the signature of the divine.

We, too, can find assurance about the word we have trusted from these two important sources. We have the testimony not only of the first generation of disciples, but of the church in every age and every nation, nearly two millennia of witnesses across six continents whose lives and legacies point to God's power at work in their lives as they, too, responded to the word that God spoke "in a Son." We also have the testimony of our own firsthand encounters with God experienced in private prayer, in worship with the community of faith, and in other movements of God's Spirit that have changed us. Like the preacher's own congregation, we also can discover firm assurance in both mind and heart that the proclamation of Christ has set us on the right course—and that we must, therefore, give our full attention and avoid the drift.

Two

Threshold Moments

(Hebrews 2:5–4:13)

When we are asked about the good that Jesus has brought into our lives, we might be tempted to answer simply with the word *salvation*. But do we regularly take the time to parse out everything that means for our lives? Do we make the time to take inventory of the deliverance Jesus has won for us and all that comes with it?

The author of Hebrews helps his hearers do this very thing as he moves forward in his sermon. Jesus has freed us from being afraid of death—and from the many ways in which our fear of our own mortality can hijack our lives and relationships (2:14-15). Jesus has pioneered for us the way to glory, giving us assurance that the promise of eternal life in God's presence is reliable (2:10). Jesus stands ever ready and willing to help us persevere in our own journey to ensure that we arrive at the goal (2:16-18).

The question remains, however: *Will* we persevere? Will we continue to trust God's promises and value Jesus's gifts sufficiently to move forward into the Christ-shaped life that leads to glory? Or will we consider the risks and the costs too great and draw ourselves back into the life we were born into not by virtue of the new birth the Holy Spirit gave us but by virtue of our very human birth into the fallen systems and structures of our society? These are questions that the preacher's hearers faced as well, and the preacher was not afraid to pose a very different counter-question: Have we sufficiently counted the costs and weighed the risks of failing to value God's promises and Jesus's gifts sufficiently?

"We See Jesus"

The preacher continues to train his audience's eyes on Jesus. He wants them to see with their mind's eye the Lord whom they serve, picturing him not as he was when he walked the dusty roads of Judea and Galilee, but as he is now, on this side of his resurrection and exaltation. Echoing Psalm 8, which speaks of the exalted place human beings enjoy over God's creation, positioned just a little bit lower than the angels (Psalm 8:5), he quotes:

> What is man, that you are mindful of him,
> or the son of man, that you care for him.
> (Psalm 8:4, Hebrews 2:6)

Modern translations like the New Revised Standard Version (NRSV) and the Common English Bible (CEB) strive, for very good reasons, for a gender-inclusive translation of "man" ("human beings" NRSV) and "son of man" ("mortals" NRSV). In this case, however, the translations obscure something that the preacher found significant, namely the phrase "son of man," which he read as a signal that the psalm said something about Jesus in particular.[1] As the psalm proceeds, then, it becomes a witness to the incarnation and exaltation of *the* Son of Man:

> You lowered him for a little while beneath the angels;
> you crowned him with glory and honor;
> you subjected all things beneath his feet.
> (Psalm 8:5-6; Hebrews 2:7-8)

The preacher admits that they do not yet see all things subjected to Jesus's authority, but they do see the one who descended to live for a little while on our level, beneath the level of the angels, and who was elevated again to "glory and honor" in his ascension to God's right hand! The completion of the first two elements of the psalm's prophetic witness to Jesus assures readers of the inevitability of the third when the present world order yields place to "the coming world" (Hebrews 2:5), God's eternal and unshakable kingdom. The preacher wants to leave his congregation, who doubtless feel despised and powerless, sure about the status, power, and ability of the one whom he will go on to present as their committed and sympathetic helper (2:16-18; 4:14-16).

The preacher wants his audience to remain focused on Jesus "crowned with glory and honor" for yet another reason: Jesus gives them a glimpse of what they may hope to be. The one who is now "crowned with glory and honor" is also "leading many sons and daughters to glory" (Hebrews 2:10). In Jesus, the psalm's vision for all humanity will be fulfilled at last, because he is our fore-runner (6:20), the pioneer (2:10; 12:2) who blazed the path to glory through costly obedience not only for himself, but for all who follow him. By showing them Jesus, the preacher has shown them that the end of their story will also be honor and glory, as they keep following the Lord who first walked through the distresses they now suffer before entering into honor forever. In so doing, he has taken their eyes off their own situation just long enough to give them the perspective they would need to return to it and persevere through it. As they see Jesus in these opening chapters, they see the exalted Lord whose honor they will share and whose aid they enjoy all along the way.

Discipleship will often mean embracing some kind of loss or deprivation. This may involve turning away from the pleasure or sense of security that comes from some sin, from economic exploitation to emotional manipulation to sexual indulgence. It may involve taking a stand that will invite ridicule, confrontation, or the loss of a job or property, even—as is regularly seen in several countries in Africa and Asia but also occasionally in the West—loss of freedom and life itself. It may involve turning away from the destiny we have chosen for ourselves and the temporal benefits that it brings and accepting a new call upon our lives from God. Whatever losses we incur as we respond to God, however, the eyes of faith, looking to Jesus, perceive "glory" in the presence of God at the end of the journey.

Grace Upon Grace

The preacher has already referred in rather general terms to the gift of "purification for sins" (1:3) and the promise of "deliverance" (1:13; 2:3) that Jesus made available to his audience. In 2:9-18, he begins to get more specific about the ways in which God in Christ has extended and continues to extend his gracious favor toward them.

"By God's gracious favor," the Son's experience of death became a source of benefit to all people (2:9). The preacher affirms that this, of course, involved making "expiation for sins" (2:17), a subject to which he will return at length in chapters 7 through 10 as he develops the theme of Jesus as our "merciful and faithful high priest." But here he focuses attention on the Son taking on our mortal flesh and blood specifically "in order that, by dying, he might destroy the one who had power over death, that is, the devil, and might free those who were enslaved their whole lives long by the fear of death" (2:14-15).

How we look upon death holds great significance for how we spend our lives. If we view it as a wall into which we slam at the end of our existence, we will remain far more fixated upon holding onto our lives in this world and all those things that represent stability, safety, and comfort in this world. That can make us slaves to our work, slaves to our image, slaves to the need to control the people close to us. It can rob us of our courage to stand up for what is just, to bear bold witness to God and God's standards, and to give ourselves away for the life of others. Fear of death, as the worm that gnaws at the core of our being, robs us of the chance to enjoy an authentic life and diverts our energies and attention from that which really can deliver us from death.[2] Yet because Jesus unwaveringly walked the path of obedience to God knowing full well that it would lead to death—and, all the more, because God responded to Jesus's obedient death by raising him to a life that death could no longer touch—he showed us that death is not a dead end, but a threshold over which we pass on the way to glory. By doing so, Jesus broke death's mystical hold over our day-to-day lives.

The Son also gives us the gift of acknowledging us as part of God's family, God's household, alongside himself. This is all the more encouraging for the preacher's audience given the Son's exalted status. He gains nothing for himself by "hobnobbing" with the many sons and daughters, but he bestows upon us a great dignity by so doing. The preacher's use of passages from the Old Testament here is striking. He places lines from Psalm 22 and Isaiah 8 on Jesus's own lips to draw out their meaning:

> The one who hallows and those who are made holy all
> share a common origin. For this reason he is not ashamed
> to call them sisters and brothers, saying,
>
> > "I will announce your name to my brothers and sisters;
> > in the midst of the assembly I will sing your praises."
>
> And again,
>
> > "I will be confident in him."
>
> And again,
>
> > "Look! Here am I along with the children God gave me!"
> > (Hebrews 2:11-13)

Jesus was remembered to have made the words of Psalm 22:1 his own at the crucifixion (Matthew 27:46; Mark 15:34), so it is perhaps natural that early Christians would ponder how the remainder of that psalm related to him. The passage from Isaiah 8:17-18, however, referred quite clearly in its original context to the prophet and his children, to whom Isaiah had given ominous names as portents of Israel's doom. The words take on a very new meaning here, with

Jesus owning his followers as family and expressing confidence in each of them that this association will not damage Jesus's honor.[3]

The preacher implicitly lays out a challenge to his congregation and, by extension, to all of us who count ourselves among "the many sons and daughters" (Hebrews 2:10). He challenges us to live up to the confidence Jesus has in us. We are invited to think about how we live, not in terms of rules, but in terms of our relationship with Jesus and doing justice to the trust he has placed in us not to put him to shame. For the first audience, this meant not disassociating themselves from Jesus on account of the pressures their neighbors were putting on them. For us, it means not betraying Jesus's confidence so as to put him to shame by our choices, our actions or inaction, or our failure to prove true disciples.

As for Jesus, the pioneer of these many sons and daughters, the preacher claims that it was "fitting" for God to bring him to glory only through suffering (2:10). What could possibly have made this "fitting"? God knew in advance the hardships through which the many sons and daughters would have to pass. God knew that the preacher's audience would have to face being shamed, mistreated, and shoved out into the margins of their society if they were going to walk the path of obeying the one God and thereby be welcomed into their eternal homeland. He knew the kinds of losses, inner wrestling, and dying to their own ambitions and dreams for their future in this world they would have to endure. And so, he set Jesus upon the same path in advance of them so that, having arrived at the goal himself, he might more sympathetically extend his help to them as they followed in the same path, ensuring that they would arrive at the same noble destination.

This would have offered significant encouragement to the preacher's congregation, as, indeed, to Christians in our present time. It speaks to the many Christians throughout our world who know suffering that is like or worse than that experienced by the first audience of this sermon. Taking forethought for the pain, deprivations, and heartache their regional authorities and neighbors would inflict upon them, the God of the universe conformed the life experience of the incarnate Son to theirs. The fact that God did not shy away from their suffering but rather set it at the very center of God's own redemptive plan might challenge us also to bravely inquire into the plight of our sisters and brothers and apply ourselves fully to supporting them in the midst of their struggle to persevere in faith.

The forethought God showed in laying out the course the Son would run speaks, however, to Christians in every setting. Do we find ourselves struggling to persevere in obedience because of the temptations either to reach for what seems pleasant or to avoid the difficult or painful? Jesus knows the force of such temptations and stands ready—with sympathy rather than condemnation in his own heart—to bring us whatever help we need to choose obedience. The preacher would agree with the words of the well-loved hymn: "Jesus knows our every weakness; / take it to the Lord in prayer."[4] Indeed, he will shortly urge his congregation that the right way to respond to the availability of Jesus's help is, simply, to take every advantage of it rather than fall short of the goal because they did not "approach the throne of favor with boldness" (4:14-16).

Failing at the Very Threshold

The preacher goes on to spend a fair amount of time considering an episode from the ancient Hebrews' desert wanderings as a narrative with direct bearing on his congregation's present situation. This episode concerns the Hebrews' failure of nerve and of trust as they stood upon the very threshold of the land God had promised to give them. The full story can be found in Numbers 14, though the preacher approaches the story first by reciting a portion of Psalm 95, a text that already applied the episode's lesson to each new generation of the faithful: "Today, if you hear God's voice, don't harden your heart!" (Psalm 95:7; Hebrews 3:7-8). Don't make the same mistake as your (spiritual) ancestors did on that fatal day in which doubt and distrust won out over faith and obedience, with disastrous results!

By the time the Hebrews arrived at the oasis of Kadesh-Barnea in the eastern Sinai wilderness, God had rescued them from slavery in Egypt, delivered them wondrously at the Red Sea, and provided food and water throughout their journey through the desert. God had given them abundant evidence of goodwill and power to deliver on God's promises. From their position south of Canaan, they sent twelve spies into the land to ascertain the nature of the forces and fortifications they would be up against, as well as to bring back samples of the land's abundant produce. When the spies returned, ten of them reported that the people of the land were too strong and their cities too well fortified for the Hebrews to have any hope of taking them. Caleb and Joshua, however, reported on the goodness of the land and their sure hope of victory, should it please God to give them the land, and urged the people not to rebel against God. The Hebrews rejected the minority report, accused God once again of bringing them out of Egypt only to destroy them, and began to make plans to return to Egypt. As a result, God swore that the entire adult population of the Hebrews would indeed die wandering in the desert on account of their distrust and disobedience.

The preacher focuses his hearers on this episode first, because he wants to use it to shape their understanding of their situation. He wants them to see themselves standing at the very threshold of their eternal inheritance, called simply to move forward to take possession of it, so that they will be all the more encouraged that perseverance is possible. One might argue that the preacher engaged in a bit of manipulation here, since his hearers in all probability had to persevere for years, even decades, further without seeing the heavenly homeland. In another sense, however, he rightly perceived them to be standing at a threshold in their own commitment to God and to one another. Each day the temptations and pressures they faced presented them with a threshold decision: Would they keep crossing over into God's future in faith, or would they look back longingly to the life and company they left behind? Understanding ourselves to stand ever at a threshold reframes our view of our situation and forces the question upon us: What do you really stand for? What are you really about? Are you for God and God's promises? Or are you for the comforts, security, and affirmation that come from the world and its promises? As soon as a person answers that question and takes a step in either direction, he or she has surely crossed a threshold in his or her spiritual walk.

The preacher also focuses on this episode from Numbers 14, however, because it mirrors his own understanding of his congregation's position, having experienced so much of God's favor and being called now to respond rightly. He uses this episode to urge them to guard their hearts against the conditions and forces that brought their spiritual ancestors to such disastrous loss at the very threshold of their own inheritance.

> Watch out, brothers and sisters, lest any one of you harbor a wickedly distrustful heart such as turns away from the living God. Rather, keep encouraging one another every day—as long as it is called "today"—in order that no one of you become hardened by sin's deceitfulness.
>
> (Hebrews 3:12-13)

Throughout his sermon the preacher catalogs his hearers' many experiences of God's generous favor and provision. Like the ancient Hebrews, they had every reason to trust God's good disposition toward them and God's reliability to continue to provide all that is needed to persevere. Distrust would, at this point, signal a serious heart defect on their part! Like the ancient Hebrews, they also faced some significant opposition. Between them and their enjoyment of God's promised goal stand some very hostile human beings. But to fear the enmity of their neighbors more than the enmity of God, to regard their neighbors' acceptance as more important than God's continued favor, and to think what they had lost more valuable than the greater joys God promised would all signal hearts that had been beguiled by sin's deceit. There were important lessons to be learned from the ancient Hebrews' heart problems.

In many parts of the world, Christians face the same or an even more fierce and costly challenge today as did the preacher's first hearers. But even in a country where Christians are scarcely persecuted, the same dangers threaten. We are constantly exposed to the beguiling voices of sin, calling us to reach for forbidden pleasures, to indulge ourselves rather than build up others, and to invest our energies in pursuits with some temporal payoff. We are faced with the grave danger of not trusting—and thus not investing ourselves fully in—God's promises to those who love and obey his Son. The promises of the society around us and the enjoyments it offers seem ever so much more real. If we yield to this spiritual sclerosis, however, we will find blockages forming in that most essential of all love relationships—our relationship with God.

Hearts That Are Fixed

The preacher urges his hearers to keep their desires trained on "the promise of entering God's rest" that lay before them (4:1). "Entering God's rest" is a major theme of Hebrews 3:7–4:11. The phrase occurs in 3:18; 4:1, 3 (twice), and 5. The word *enter* on its own appears in Hebrews 3:19; 4:6 (twice). The author wants to impress this goal firmly in his hearers' minds, so that they will measure their success or failure in this life solely in terms of whether or not they remain in line with that goal and so that all their energies will be focused afresh on attaining it. The promise that still lies before us does not concern some parcel of land in the eastern Mediterranean region. Neither is it merely the experience of rest or inner peace in the midst of this life. The preacher speaks here of "God's rest" to refer to the same goal described elsewhere in the sermon as the heavenly homeland

(11:16), the abiding city (13:14), the unshakable kingdom (12:28), "heaven itself" (9:24), the divine realm beyond the visible heavens, into which Jesus has already entered as our forerunner (6:19-20), whom we follow into glory (2:8-10). The apostle Paul firmly believed no investment or sacrifice in this life to be too great for the sake of attaining the glory of life in God's eternity (2 Corinthians 4:16-18). Far from trivializing our experiences in this life, however, the promise of entering God's rest magnifies the importance of how we choose to invest ourselves each and every day. In the words of the Anglican priest and poet John Donne, "upon every minute of this life, depend millions of years in the next."[5]

We will avoid the hardening of our hearts if, in the words of a collect in *The Book of Common Prayer*, "our hearts may surely there be fixed where true joys are to be found," if our hearts and, with them, our wills remain responsive first and foremost to what God has given us and what God has promised yet to grant us.[6] Such a "fixed heart" impels its owner to move forward in trust in the face of any difficulty, rather than succumb to temptation.

Two Essential Resources for Faithful Perseverance

The preacher's audience experienced significant forces in their lives and circumstances that made it difficult for their hearts to remain "fixed" on God's gifts and promises. These forces exerted themselves in very practical, very immediate ways. Neighbors would ridicule them and the hope that had drawn them away from their former commitments and practices. They were without customers, without advocates, without influence. They found themselves paying a significant cost in the "here and now" for the sake of shadowy promises of something that might materialize in the "there and then." And, at the same time, they still faced every human temptation to reach for forbidden pleasures, to secure their own advantage at another's expense, and to indulge their ego rather than yield to the Holy Spirit.

The preacher encourages them to make the most of two powerful resources for combatting these forces that threatened to dislodge their hearts from remaining fixed upon God's good purposes. The first of these resources is, simply, each other! He commissions the group as a whole to exercise vigilance over each of its members and to invest themselves in one another's successful perseverance. In this passage he calls them to offer persistent encouragement to one another (3:12-13); elsewhere in his sermon he lifts up material assistance and displays of solidarity with those who are suffering the greatest discouragement or abuse (6:9-10; 10:32-34; 13:1-3, 16). He urges his hearers to take up eagerly and in all seriousness their responsibility to one another as members of a new family. The preacher knows the power of social reinforcement, and he has much to teach those of us who naively believe too strongly in the power of the individual and his or her will. The negative power of their neighbors to dissuade them from persevering in gratitude and faithfulness to God was already making itself known as some believers began to withdraw from the group (10:25). Those who remained had to ramp up their investment in one another to counteract this force.

We deprive ourselves and one another of a great resource when we believe the lie that faith or religion is a private matter. Nothing could be further from a scripture-shaped vision for the church, whereby we are mobilized to offer one another consistent support, encouragement, and accountability. When I hear a friend speak openly of how he or she has encountered God and experienced God's presence and movement in life, I am strengthened and confirmed in my own experience of God. Similarly, my sisters and brothers need the encouragement that comes from hearing how God has helped me in a given situation, how he has strengthened me to overcome temptation, or how he has made his presence and direction known when I needed it.

As we share testimonies with each other, and with brothers and sisters around the globe, about how God has proven reliable in our collective experience, we diminish the possibility that distrust will harden any one of our hearts. As we remind one another of the reliability of God's prescriptions for a full and authentic life, we counteract the persuasive power of the voices that persistently suggest that the temporary pleasures life offers are more worthy of our time, energy, and ambition than the pleasure of following God with a whole heart. As our brothers and sisters take the risk of helping us see where we have been beguiled by the enticements of a particular sin, they offer us a lifeline back to clear thinking in the light of our shared goal of pursuing God's best future for us.

The second resource the preacher mentions is, of course, the Word that still speaks. The preacher probably has more in mind here than the written legacy of the scriptures. He would include scripture, of course, but also any means by which we might "hear God's voice" speaking to us—that voice against which we must not harden our hearts (3:7, 15). The word of God, like a sword able to cleave through a body and lay bare its innards, lays bare the health or the disease of our hearts (4:12). When we hear God's word, do we trust, obey, and line up our lives accordingly? If so, our heart is shown to be healthy. Do we, conversely, distance ourselves from the word, try to protect our current lifestyles and investments, and blunt its impact? If so, we have serious heart problems, and we need the help of our sisters and brothers all the more.

"As I Swore in My Wrath"

Some people find the God whom they encounter in the Old Testament to be very different from the God proclaimed in the New Testament. You may have heard verbal thumbnail portraits like, "The Old Testament God is a God of Law, but the New Testament God is one of grace," or, "The God of the Old Testament is a God of anger, but the God of the New Testament is a God of love." People who promote such dichotomies show thereby that they haven't really read *either* the Old or New Testament very carefully! God's character is, rather, remarkably consistent from beginning to end. God loves God's creatures *and* God expects to be honored by God's creatures—and holds them accountable when this honor is withheld! "Eternal judgment," one of the focal topics in the basic instruction that the preacher's audience had received (Hebrews 6:2), is one of the realities most universally affirmed across the New Testament.

The preacher is not at all embarrassed by God's anger. He can quote Old Testament passages selectively when it suits him. He does not omit the phrases in Psalm 95 that speak of God being "angry at that generation" that God led out from Egypt and who later provoked God on the threshold of the promised land nor does he omit the phrases that speak of God promising on oath "in God's anger" that they would never enter God's rest (Psalm 95:10-11; Hebrews 3:10-11, 17; 4:3). God's potential for anger is, for the preacher, a fact with which to reckon, not a theological relic of a less enlightened time to be explained away.

In the particular situation described in Psalm 95, God's anger was readily intelligible. God had already worked great wonders for the benefit of the ancient Hebrews and had given them every assurance that God would continue to favor them—and had the power and good will to do so. The ancient Hebrews' rebellion at the threshold of Canaan was born from their slight regard for what God had done for them in the years leading up to that moment, their distrust of God's good will toward them and God's power to deliver on God's word, and their greater regard for the threat posed by human beings, should the Israelites move forward to confront them, than the threat posed by God, should they dishonor and disobey God. The Greek philosopher Aristotle, an astute observer of human behavior among many other things, wrote that people "are angry when they are insulted by people whom they think ought to treat them well; an example would be people on whom they had showed favor or were currently showing favor . . . or desired to show favor."[7] God's response to the desert generation was readily understandable indeed.

For the preacher, however, the danger of provoking God to anger did not belong only to the distant past of the "Old Testament." He will shortly present it as a lively possibility for any members among his congregation who might have thought that their neighbors' favor was more valuable than God's, and who, by pulling away from the Christian group, would bear public witness to their neighbors that Jesus's friendship and favor were not worth the cost of keeping them.

> For if we continue sinning willfully after receiving knowledge of the truth, there no longer remains any sacrifice for sins—only the fear-inspiring prospect of judgment and of a fire that is eager to consume the adversaries. A person who sets aside Moses' Law dies without mercy on the testimony of two or three witnesses. Of how much worse punishment do you think the person who has trampled God's Son underfoot . . . and insulted the Spirit of favor will be found to deserve? For we know the One who said,
>
> "Vengeance belongs to me; I will repay";
>
> and again,
>
> "The Lord will judge his people."
>
> It is a fearsome thing to fall into the hands of the living God! (Hebrews 10:26-31)

The author primarily seeks to evoke gratitude on the part of his hearers which will lead them to continue to honor God and the Son in their words and actions. He is not at all reluctant, however, to pursue a secondary strategy of evoking fear of the consequences of failing to pursue the path gratitude properly requires.

This aspect of the preacher's thinking is related to his conviction that the Son of God has *initiated* a relationship with him and his congregation, a relationship in which they must continue to respond honorably in keeping with the Son's grace toward them. It is also related to his conviction that the Son has set them on a journey toward ultimate and eternal deliverance, but it is also a summons to keep moving forward. They must remain faithful and obedient to this relationship, this summons, "in order that no one fall after the same pattern of disobedience" that the ancient Hebrews manifested (Hebrews 4:11). Thus, the preacher can reassure his congregation that "we are Christ's household" but also add the proviso: "if we hold onto our boldness and to the boast that our hope provides" (3:6). He can encourage them that "we have become partners with Christ," the exalted Son at God's right hand, but add the condition: "if we hold our first confidence firm to the end" (3:14). It may strike us as problematic that the preacher regards our continued enjoyment of our place in God's household as conditional. Strong theological currents since the Reformation have sought to minimize or negate altogether what human efforts contribute to our salvation, our arrival at God's good ends for us. Those currents, however, must not be allowed to drown out the very words of scripture.

The preacher leaves us with a frightening image: "And there is no creature hidden from his view, but all are naked with their throats pulled back before the eyes of the One to whom we must give account" (4:13). We are not allowed to lose sight of the fact that we are all accountable to God and that being accounted "just" or "righteous" in our dealings with God—including our submission to God's purposes and design for us and our fidelity in our relationship with our Creator and Redeemer—is of paramount and ultimate importance to our eternal well-being. Trusting Jesus does not eliminate our accountability before God, as both Jesus and Paul would affirm (see, for example, Matthew 7:21-23; 2 Corinthians 5:9-10; Galatians 6:7-8); trusting Jesus only changes the nature of it. Have we responded well to the favor and the deliverance offered by God's Son? Have we given this "way out" from our former sins and "way back" to living righteously before God the attention that it deserves? Have we allowed the Son's commitment to and investment in us to arouse commitment and investment to match, such that the whole orientation of our lives has been changed in a Godward direction?

We are still responsible before God for how we have made use of God's gifts and responded to God's grace. It is therefore *always* advantageous to us, in the present time, to listen for the word that God would speak to us, whether in scripture, in prayer, in the Spirit, or in the sister or brother, and prove ourselves pliable in response. Submitting to God's word now about what we are committing or omitting will position us to hear God's word of affirmation and welcome in the end.

Three

Responding Gracefully to Grace

(Hebrews 4:14–6:20)

Some Christians talk about God's grace and the gift of salvation as if we were essentially *receptacles*—boxes that either have or have not received something from God. The author of Hebrews would not approve of this image. Rather, he wants us to understand that where God's grace and favor are concerned, we are *soil*. The question is not merely what we have received, but what effects God's grace has generated in us and through us. Have we proven to be fruitful soil, bringing forth and offering back to God the witness and the service God's gifts merit? Do the fruits of our lives show us to have given the highest value to the favor of God and of the Son?

Even as the preacher challenges his hearers to be certain that their investments of themselves reflect properly and proportionately the value of God's gifts—a tall order in any century or setting—he assures them that proving to be the fruitful soil that "receives a blessing from God" (6:7) is entirely feasible. For they have the unfailing promises of God on which to rely (6:13-20) and an unfailing mediator who will reliably connect them to the resources they need to persevere in the path of grateful response in the face of any resistance (4:14-16).

A Sympathetic and Unfailing Mediator

The preacher left his hearers with a fear-inspiring image as he closed his reflections on the failure of the ancient Hebrews in the desert and the implications of their sorry example for his congregation (Hebrews 4:11-13). He opens a new segment of his sermon with words crafted to encourage and inspire confidence, for such confidence is required to continue moving forward in faithful obedience in light of God's gracious provisions:

> Having therefore a great high priest who has passed through the heavens—Jesus, the Son of God—let us hold firm to what we profess. For we don't have a high priest who is unable to sympathize with our weaknesses, but one who has been tested in every way as we are, without sinning. Let's keep drawing close to the throne of favor with boldness, in order that we may receive mercy and find favor for timely help. (Hebrews 4:14-16)

One the greatest gifts that God has given us, the preacher urges, is a sympathetic and unfailing mediator, one who will always secure for his followers what they need in order to press on toward God's good ends for them. Through him, we can approach God with boldness and receive help. He has already announced this earlier in his sermon (2:16-18) and will dwell on the quality and achievement of Jesus's priestly mediation at length as the sermon develops (7:1–10:18). Our enjoyment of such a mediator is the foundation for perseverance (10:19-25). The preacher reminds the members of the congregation that they were not left on their own to grit their teeth and push forward. They had open access to the God who would supply them with whatever resources they needed to persevere in the face of hostility and hardship, whether the inner resources of spiritual strength, assurance, and comfort or the external resources of material aid, loving care, and encouragement from their fellow believers in response to God's mobilization of God's own gifts. They simply needed to keep drawing near and asking God for the "timely help" they required with the boldness that the Son's mediation gave them. Drawing near to God would keep them drawing near to one another (rather than shrinking back into the society of their neighbors) and drawing nearer to their eternal homeland.

Priests played an important role in both Jewish and Greco-Roman religion, standing between human beings and God or the gods to build or repair bridges between the two, assure the favor of the divine toward the people, and secure for the people the assistance that only God or the gods could provide. There is an almost universal instinct among human cultures that there are great powers above us and that these powers, these holy others, have to be approached in just the right way in order to harness their power for our benefit and not our destruction. Similarly universal, therefore, is the figure of the mediator who has the proper knowledge of how to accomplish this. As the preacher rightly observes, these mediators were chosen, usually in some way that signaled that the choice was made by the *divine* party; they were not simply volunteers (Hebrews 5:4-5).

We may be accustomed to thinking about Jesus as "our Prophet, Priest, and King,"[1] but the idea of Jesus as a priest—indeed, as the ultimate high priest between God and humankind—was only just being forged as the writer of Hebrews crafted this sermon. The preacher is painfully aware that Jesus lacked some of the most basic qualifications for priesthood articulated in the scriptures, such as descent from the patriarch Levi. He found evidence for Jesus's special appointment to priesthood, however, in the psalms, indeed, in the very psalm that spoke of the Son's exaltation to God's right hand (Psalm 110:1, recited in Hebrews 1:13). As God's speech to the Son continued in the words of that psalm, God further declared, "You are a priest forever in the line of Melchizedek" (Psalm 110:4; Hebrews 5:6). Speaking of Jesus as acting now in the capacity of high priest on our behalf is the preacher's way of expressing Jesus's ongoing commitment to and connection with us. Jesus is not merely "at God's right hand," to borrow from Paul, Jesus is "at God's right hand, *interceding for us*" (Romans 8:34, emphasis added). Though at

God's right hand, Jesus is still actively investing himself in those who have entrusted themselves to him.

The Son of God's priesthood has all the advantages of the high priests appointed under the old covenant with none of the disadvantages. The preacher thinks it important that a mediator be sympathetic toward the weaknesses and failures of those on whose behalf he or she intercedes. The high priests serving in the tabernacle and, later, the temple, were inclined to be sympathetic because they had the same weaknesses and failings. Hence the first offering made by such high priests on the Day of Atonement was for their own sins and those of their households (Hebrews 5:2-3; see Leviticus 16:6, 15-16). The Son, while he learned sympathy for human weakness through his experiences of being "tested in every way as we are" (Hebrews 4:15) during the years in which he shared our flesh and blood (2:14; 5:7), nevertheless consistently gave God the obedience that was God's due. In other words, he remained "without sin" (4:15). There are thus no obstacles in the relationship between the Son and the Father for which the former must make amends before he is in a position to intercede on behalf of others. The preacher offers Jesus's unique combination of sympathy and sinlessness to his congregation as the basis for complete confidence that God will favorably receive them and supply what they need to remain faithful, since they have such an incomparable mediator working on their behalf.

The preacher paints a powerful sketch of the character of the experiences that taught the Son such sympathy for his many sisters and brothers. These experiences led the Son himself to "offer prayers and pleas with loud outcries and tears to the One who was able to deliver him out from death" (Hebrews 5:7). This verse has led many readers to think about Jesus's prayer in the garden of Gethsemane, where Jesus asked to be spared the brutal death that loomed before him yet, in the end, committed himself to persevere in the path that had been marked out for him. The preacher, however, may not be thinking of a single incident in Jesus's life but of the quality of the whole, over the course of which Jesus had many occasions to wrestle with God in order to find the strength to commit to moving forward—a life of "learning obedience through what he experienced" (5:8).

Many translations represent the opening phrase of Hebrews 5:8, "although he was a Son," as a condition that qualifies what follows:

> Although he was a Son, he learned obedience through what he suffered (NRSV).

> Son though he was, he learned obedience from what he suffered (NIV).

> Although he was a Son, he learned obedience from what he suffered (CEB).

The preacher will assert later in his sermon, however, that enduring suffering for the sake of character formation is exactly what every son or daughter should *expect* as a result of being a genuine son or daughter in a family (12:7-8). Though it cuts against the grain of standard translations, it may be truer to the preacher's meaning to understand "although he was a Son" to qualify what comes *before* it.[2] God heard (and answered) Jesus's prayers and pleas because of the reverent fear that Jesus exhibited; that is, God responded because of Jesus's virtuous disposition and not merely because of the family connection he enjoyed uniquely with God.

The preacher's portrait of Jesus as a person of prayer assures his congregation that Jesus knows intimately what it feels like to face the pressures and pains that they face (and far more besides!). They can be all the more assured of his sympathetic intercession for them before God. But it also provides them (and us) with a model of how to approach the throne of grace in the midst of those pressures and pains. The preacher shows Jesus standing in the tradition of the psalmists who gave ancient Israel and the early church a vocabulary for prayer that included the expression of anger, fear, desperation, and even the starkest doubt. The Son teaches us, the "many sons and daughters," how to endure in the face of the most dire challenges to faithful perseverance. Prayer does not need to be polite. It needs, rather, to be honest. If we open ourselves up fully to God, God will encounter us in the depths of our being where we most need to find God's "timely help." The challenges that drive us to our knees become thereby opportunities to "learn obedience." It is important for us to notice in this regard that Jesus's endurance of suffering is not the result of his prayer being deficient or God's being absent. Jesus models how to pray with a view to persevering *through* suffering and difficulty, not with a view to escaping it. The challenges we encounter exercise us in our commitment to God and our investment of ourselves in following God, strengthening our God-directed orientation. In this way, we will be enabled to keep moving forward toward the eternal deliverance that God has opened up for us.

A Summons to Responsibility

The preacher interrupts his own flow at this point to do what many preachers, perhaps, have wished themselves able to do: stop in the middle of the sermon, look up, and ask, "Are you all paying attention out there?" The preacher questions whether his listeners are ready to receive the rather involved teaching concerning Jesus's death and ascension that he will set out for them in the chapters that follow.

> For indeed, although you ought to be teachers yourselves
> by this late date, you stand in need of someone else to keep
> teaching you the foundational principles of God's oracles,
> and you have become as people needing milk and not solid
> food! (Hebrews 5:12)

The preacher expresses the expectation that people will continue to grow in their faith to the point that they themselves begin to take on responsibility to help others grow in faith, rather than remaining forever on the receiving end of such nourishment. We do not know how long his listeners have been followers of Jesus, but it has been long enough, in the preacher's estimation, for them to have made considerably more progress in this regard than they have been showing.

The preacher may regard the withdrawal of some members from this Christian community (10:25) as evidence for this general lack of taking responsibility. Why did the others not rally to stop their defection? Why did they not assume the role of "teachers," reminding their wavering sisters and brothers of all they had received from God through the Son, and of all that they looked forward to receiving? Why did they not warn them of the dangers of thinking too little of the Son's gifts and too lightly of the Son's honor? Was their own foundation so inadequately laid that they had not risen to the level of maturity and responsibility the preacher could have expected by this point?

Since the preacher will go on shortly to share this "long and difficult" teaching about Jesus anyway (7:1–10:18) and since he does entrust them with one another's perseverance throughout the sermon (3:12-13; 6:9-10; 10:23-25; 12:14-17; 13:1-3), he clearly believes them to be up to the task. But he reprimands them here for not having taken sufficient responsibility for one another up to this point.

The images of "milk" and "solid food" (or "meat") are common in Greco-Roman discussions about education. Metaphors of feeding, of ingestion and digestion, are indeed singularly appropriate. As new believers, we are taught the basics of the gospel and the way of life that honors God. As we drink this in and let it form our lives, we change and grow—just like milk and soft foods enable a baby to gain weight and develop as he or she makes the nutrients and calories his or her "own." But as we grow, we inherit greater responsibilities, from the responsibility to heed the increasingly advanced instructions from our parents, to the responsibility to look out for our younger siblings when our parents are out of the room, to the responsibility to help our parents in the management of the home—eventually to the responsibility of becoming parents ourselves.

The preacher expects that Christ-followers will follow a similar path toward maturity. Conversion, baptism, initial instruction in the faith, and reception into a congregation are all part of the "larval stage" of a great, ongoing process of metamorphosis, in which we are impelled forward more and more toward Christlikeness and greater responsibility to assist one another on that journey. The preacher summons his hearers to "move forward to perfection" (6:1), a term that suggests arriving at the final state of a process, very much as creatures move from the starting point of birth to maturity. He urges us to allow the teachings and experiences of God we have already received to shape our lives and to drive us on to greater and greater growth, commitment, and fruitfulness.

We have many opportunities to take up our responsibility as Christians who are no longer "infants" in the faith. One major area involves the training of our youth in the faith, whether through involvement in teaching Sunday school, one-on-one mentoring, or taking an active role in youth programs. Another important area involves the support and encouragement of sisters and brothers facing difficulty, whether locally or globally, through our prayers, our personal connections with them, and our sharing what we have so that they experience the love of the family of God in real and needed ways. Each one of us can make an important contribution to another Christian's ability to hold onto God in the midst of hardship. And when a brother or sister is in danger of damaging the integrity of his or her walk and throwing aside eternal rewards for the "temporary pleasure of sin" (11:25), we can help that one recover his or her vision—just as we will likely need such assistance at some point ourselves!

One of John Wesley's basic strategies for encouraging Christian growth, both in terms of withdrawing from all that would displease our divine Benefactor and in terms of pursuing all that would please him, was the "class meeting." This was essentially a small group comprised of Christians who genuinely desired to make progress toward holiness and did not shy from the difficult work that it would entail. This included allowing others to lay their own hearts bare, assisting others in seeing past their own self-deceptions, and helping one another keep their attention and best efforts consistently fixed on moving closer and closer to the mark of scriptural holiness. Whatever form they take in contemporary Christianity, such regular and intentional encounters with one another have the potential to provide significant support for our journey forward into greater maturity as disciples.

A Fruitful Return

The preacher's congregation had only one viable option: allowing themselves to be carried along to maturity (Hebrews 6:1), directing all of their efforts toward entering God's rest (4:11), holding firmly to their confession (4:14), and continuing to draw near to God's throne for the assistance needed to persevere. Any alternative, according to the preacher, was unthinkable in every respect:

> For those who had once been enlightened and experienced the heavenly gift and had a share in the Holy Spirit and experienced the good word of God and the powers of the coming age and, after all that, fall away can't possibly be restored to repentance, since they are hoisting God's Son up on the cross all over again to their own harm and exposing him to public disgrace. For ground that drinks up the rain repeatedly falling upon it and brings forth crops useful for those on whose behalf it is being cultivated receives God's blessing. But if it produces thorns and thistles, it is shown to be unfit and well-nigh accursed—its end is burning. (6:4-8)

This is perhaps the most disputed passage in Hebrews, largely because it is often approached from the standpoint of the interpreter's theological convictions and not from the standpoint of the preacher's and his audience's cultural values. The passage is often drawn into arguments about whether or not we can "lose our salvation," with defenders of the position of "eternal security" (that is, "once saved, always saved") finding ways to claim that the preacher is not talking here about genuine Christians. The preacher, however, could never frame the question this way since, for him, "salvation" is what he himself looks forward to receiving at Christ's coming again (1:14; 9:28). He looks at Christian life quite differently—and in terms that made very good sense to him and to his congregation.

The logic of this passage is rooted in the dynamics of reciprocity, the expectations surrounding the giving and receiving of gifts, where *gifts* refers not to trinkets and white elephants, but to meaningful and often needed resources, assistance, or intervention. It was common knowledge in the first century that to accept such a gift was also to accept an obligation to the giver. The greater the gift or assistance given (the "grace" shown), the greater was the obligation to show gratitude. Between two people, the giving and receiving of a gift involved more than the transfer of a commodity. It initiated a relationship that would continue to be refreshed as the recipient made a return of some kind, prompting future gifts or assistance, which would then be reciprocated, and so on. These relationships tended to form long-lasting alliances. Where one party in the relationship was significantly inferior to the other in terms of resources, political influence, and the like, he or she could still make an appropriate return in the form of increasing the reputation of the giver, showing loyalty toward the giver, and looking for opportunities to perform services for the giver. The two parties might not exchange gifts of anything approaching equal value, but they could each show equal commitment to the *relationship*.

Grace (*charis*, in Greek) was not a particularly religious word in the first-century Roman empire. It was an everyday word most typically used in the context of relationships between people who were bound to each other by mutual favor and assistance of some kind. Grace was well received only when it produced a grateful spirit and nurtured a relationship of loyalty and mutual assistance. For someone to accept favor and gifts and later insult the giver, break faith with him or her, or refuse him or her a service would be unthinkable. It would brand that person an ingrate, someone who should never expect a restoration to favor. The preacher's hearers would have been well-schooled long before their conversion in these basic ethical principles:

> "Not to return gratitude for benefits is a disgrace, and the whole world counts it as such." (Seneca)[3]

> "Those who insult their benefactors will by nobody be esteemed to deserve a favor." (Dio Chrysostom)[4]

When it came to God or the gods, the dynamics were no different than among human beings. Indeed, their significantly greater gifts and their greater honor simply made a grateful return all the more necessary and the consequences of ingratitude all the more inescapable.[5]

In Hebrews 6:4-8, then, the preacher does not try to describe people who "have been saved" or not. He describes people upon whom the God of the universe has lavished gift after gift, grace upon grace. These people, which include his audience, have been favored with knowledge of God's truth. For Jewish converts, this would include the truth of what God had done in and for Jesus, the Messiah; for Gentile converts, this would include the truth of who God was in the first place, ending the alienation from the living God they had experienced when they were carried away in the worship of the images of counterfeit gods. They experienced the gift of the Holy Spirit, whose presence assured them of their adoption into God's family as the "many sons and daughters" (Hebrews 2:10, see also Galatians 4:6-7) and empowered them to live righteous and holy lives beyond the power of their fleshly inclinations (see Galatians 5:16-25). They received God's "good word" (Hebrews 6:5), God's promises to them, affirmed for them by the same Spirit. They experienced some foretaste of the age to come, perhaps in their collective experiences of God's presence in worship and perhaps in some other supernatural manifestations (see 2:3-4). They have been like "ground drinking up the rain repeatedly falling upon it" (6:7), having experienced shower after shower of God's favor.

For such people now to withdraw, to walk away from the household of faith that God was drawing together, to confess to their neighbors (whether verbally or implicitly by their change in practice) that it was better to fit in and enjoy their good graces than continue to endure their hostility for the sake of some intangible homeland would mean bringing Jesus into further disrepute in the world instead of upholding his honor. It would be to put him on the cross all over again—this time not in ignorance of who he is, but willfully shaming the Son of God (6:6). It doesn't matter how one might describe this action, whether as "drifting off" (2:1), "neglecting so great a deliverance" (2:2-3), "turning away from the living God" (3:12), "falling short" (4:1; 12:15), or "falling away" (6:6). It all stems from a value judgment that sets a higher premium on the world's favor and friendship than on God's, and a greater insult to God can scarcely be imagined.

The preacher has been reminding his hearers all along of the ways in which God has invested in them, providing the good things they now have in their lives and promising hope for the future because of the connection the Son has made with them. The message of Hebrews 6:4-8 is that God's great and varied gifts must produce the good fruits of grateful service in those whom God has benefited. It would be unthinkable to meet God's generous and persistent cultivation of the soil of the hearers' lives with actions that would insult and alienate the Giver. The agricultural analogy drives this point home. God sends the rains upon the earth for a purpose, and the ground makes good use of God's "gift" of rain only if it brings forth a particular "return." The Son's investment of his life to bring them good, an investment in which he went "all in," should not result in a return of disdain and disloyalty! In an interesting twist of the typical use of agricultural imagery to speak about benefaction and gratitude, the preacher speaks of his hearers as soil that has been cultivated not for the sake of the cultivator, but for the sake of others.[6] What God seeks most from them in return for his own investment in them is their investment in each other, sustaining one another along the difficult path of faithfulness in their hostile environment.

The preacher quickly goes on to assure his hearers that he thinks and expects only the best of them:

> But we have been convinced where you're concerned, beloved, that better things—things leading to deliverance—await you, even though we are speaking this way. For God is not unjust to overlook your labor and the love that you have shown in God's name as you served the saints and continue to serve them. But we desire that each one of you continue to show the same eager investment of yourselves in connection with the certainty that hope gives, even to the very end—so that you will not become sluggish, but rather imitators of those who, through trust and perseverance, are inheriting what was promised. (6:9-12)

Some Christian traditions, including those in the Wesleyan tradition, place a good deal of emphasis on "assurance," the inner testimony that tells us we belong to God. When the preacher wishes to give his hearers assurance, he points them to the degree to which they had devoted (and are continuing to devote) themselves to living as grateful recipients of God's favor. They had proven themselves to be good ground thus far in their journey. They had allowed God's grace toward them to achieve its desired effects to date as they have brought forth crop after crop of doing good on behalf of their sisters and brothers (6:7)! They had been putting themselves out in serving one another, helping one another persevere (6:10). When some of their number had been harder hit by their neighbors or the local authorities, the rest stood with them and supported them, even though it meant that they were painting targets on their own backs (10:32-34). They had remained bold in their association with the name of Jesus and with the people called out in his name. They had maintained justice in their relationship with God and the Son of God by responding to divine favor in ways that brought honor to the name of Jesus and offered service in the name of Jesus. And God, who is supremely just, had surely recognized this and would continue to respond favorably to those who, while they might not have been worthy to receive favor in the first place, have worthily received favor by responding to it (so far!) in ways that showed they appreciated its matchless value. The preacher thus encourages his hearers to continue investing themselves and their resources in one another, putting themselves out to ensure one another's perseverance in faith and obedience to the gospel message. The love, service, and support we give other Christians is translated into "principal" that can never be diminished, for it is held in trust in the mind of God, "who is not unjust to overlook" such service to the saints.

This has bearing on several of the exhortations the preacher has already made. They can indeed have confidence as they approach God's throne of favor, assured that God will continue to assist them on their journey (4:14-16), "because God is not unjust to overlook" the investments they themselves have made in response to God's investment in them. They have every reason to persevere in trust and, therefore, to "make every effort to enter God's rest" (3:7–4:11), because "God is not unjust to overlook" the loyalty and the service they have shown thus far in response to God's initiating favor. Their pious concern for not bringing Jesus's name into disdain among their unbelieving neighbors will keep them moving forward in the right direction. Likewise, their awareness that they have been responding nobly to God, whose gifts can never be outmatched, will help them persevere after the sermon ends and they leave the safety of the circle of believers to face the challenges awaiting them among their neighbors in their cities.

In this context, there was no danger that they would have misunderstood this as "earning their salvation" by doing good works for one another. Their lives were simply being transformed by God's grace as they responded to God's grace, allowing gratitude toward God to shape their daily choices and investments of themselves. It remains a picture of grace from beginning to end: God initiates the movement with God's own, boundless generosity toward us; we respond to God's gifts by letting them have their full effect in us and, through us, in one another.

Before moving on, it may be appropriate to consider some limits on this passage's application. In the long history of the church, some have appealed to this passage to exclude from repentance believers who have fallen into some serious sin. Do not believers who commit egregious sins bring disgrace upon the name of Christ? Have they not brought forth the spiritual equivalent of "thorns and thistles" (6:8) in response to God's generous showers of favor upon them?

The preacher took God's grace very seriously and warned his congregation strenuously against taking God's grace for granted. God is not simply a vast supply of grace upon which we draw at our will and convenience; God is a Being who decides whether, and under what circumstances, to show favor or hold to strict account. But the preacher is also addressing these words to believers before they have made the serious mistakes that he fears they might make, and he does so specifically in order to help them keep making the choices that will honor God and sustain the Christian community and its witness. He does not address penitent believers who have fallen away and wish to return to the community of faith. We cannot assume that, if some of those Christians who had already withdrawn from Christian gatherings (10:25) sought to return, he would have told them that it was impossible for them to renew their repentance (see 6:4). We do know, however, that numerous other New Testament authors faced the specific problem of believers who had strayed into serious error or sin and that their counsel was for the stronger disciples to seek to restore them to the right path (see, for example, Galatians 6:1-2; James 5:19-20; 1 John 1:9–2:2; 5:14-17; Jude 22-23). While, then, on the one hand, we should be careful never to take God's favor for granted and seek in every situation to act with a view to honoring, showing loyalty to, and advancing the interests of our divine Bene-factor, we also cannot presume to know or to set limits on God's willingness to extend favor afresh to the truly penitent.

What More Can God Say?

The preacher will say a great deal more later in his sermon about what it means to "be imitators of those who, through trust and perse-verance, are inheriting what was promised" (6:12). What is prob-ably the most celebrated and familiar portion of this New Testament book—the "faith chapter" (chapter 11)—outlines what persevering trust looks like in action, holding up a veritable "cloud of witnesses" (12:1) for imitation and encouragement. At this point, it is enough for the preacher to recall one example, perhaps the paramount example of trust and perseverance: Abraham. In particular, however, the preacher is interested for now in what gave Abraham such confi-dence, empowering him to leave his homeland behind in the certain hope of "a better, that is, a heavenly homeland" (11:16).

The preacher focuses on a particularly remarkable feature of God's promise to bless Abraham, namely that God did not merely make a promise. God added a solemn oath to the promise. Taking oaths was a common practice in the ancient world. Oaths were taken in the courtroom to guarantee truth-telling on the part of a witness, for the oath invokes a god's honor that no lies would be told (and, thus, invited divine punishment if the god's name was abused). Oaths were taken in connection with agreements with the same dynamics undergirding them. The preacher is correct that an oath carried great weight toward the resolution of uncertainty (6:16).

The preacher notices that God had used an oath formula when

God renewed the promise to Abraham: "So help me, I will bless you and I will multiply your descendants to become as the stars of heaven or the sand beside the shore of the sea, and your offspring shall inherit the cities of your enemies" (Genesis 22:17). God, who is the "Amen," the truth itself, does not deceive. But God was so keen on giving Abraham cause for confident trust that God not only made a promise but added an oath on top of it. God could not have staked God's own honor on delivering the goods more forcefully or clearly.

This was not, however, a special kindness that God showed Abraham only. The preacher has discovered, through his close and careful examination of the Scriptures, that God has done precisely the same for him and for all who have drawn near to God through God's Son.

> God, desiring all the more abundantly to indicate to the heirs of the promise the unchangeable character of his purpose, interposed an oath—in order that by means of two unalterable things (in regard to which it is impossible that God should prove false) we who have fled might have firm confidence to hold onto the hope set before us.
>
> (Hebrews 6:17-18)

The preacher does not clearly indicate what these two things are. One of them, however, surely involves a different oath God has taken in regard to the mediator God has provided for us, Jesus, the Son of God. The preacher leaves the hearers in suspense about this oath for now. In the very next chapter, however, he will make a great deal of this oath and the bearing it has on the confidence we can have in Jesus to connect us now and forever with God's favor and promised end:

> "The Lord has sworn and will not change his mind: 'You are a priest forever in the line of Melchizedek'."
>
> (Psalm 110:4; Hebrews 7:20-21)

The promise that this oath upholds might be the other Old Testament passage that will play such a large role in the central section of this sermon, specifically, the promise connected with the new covenant announced in Jeremiah 31:31-34 and quoted in Hebrews 8:7-13. This promise has to do with the decisive removal of all that keeps human beings at arm's length from the holy God, thus fitting them to enter God's eternal presence forever. The oath upholds the new priesthood, Jesus's priesthood, by means of which that covenant with its promises becomes reality.

The first stanza of the widely sung hymn "How Firm a Foundation, Ye Saints of the Lord" captures the force of the preacher's argument well:

> What more can he say than to you he has said,
> To you, who for refuge to Jesus have fled?[7]

They should have every confidence, like Abraham and Sarah themselves, that "the one who promised is reliable" (10:23; 11:11) and so continue to respond faithfully and obediently to the God who calls them to inherit eternity. The preacher, like the hymn writer, looks to the Scriptures to find the pronouncements of God that have the potential to provide assurance sufficient to withstand the onslaught of doubts within and hostility without as Christ's followers press on in faithfulness. His example shows them to be the ancient oracles in which we still hear God's living voice, if we continue to listen for that voice in them. The solid foundation in which our hope is grounded is the reliability of the One who promised, making that hope itself something far more solid than wishful thinking. Our hope, bound to the *object* of our hope, the eternal realm of God's presence, becomes a strong tether that binds us, even while in the midst of the storms of this present life, to the anchorage of God's realm.

The preacher returns at this point to the person of Jesus, the topic from which he had broken off to shake up his congregation a bit (5:11). Just as Jesus's resurrection is the assurance of our own (see

1 Corinthians 15:20-22), Jesus's entrance into the heavenly realm at his ascension is the assurance that his followers will also surely arrive "where Jesus went as our forerunner" (6:20). The Christian hope is not for some unprecedented action on God's part; Jesus's presence at God's right hand is the proof of the viability of our hope. And as his followers keep their connection with Jesus secure through their faithful witness and service, their hope also remains surely planted on the other side of the veil which obscures the unshakable, invisible realm from our earthly sight.

Four

A Full, Perfect, and Sufficient Sacrifice

(Hebrews 7:1–10:18)

At the center of Hebrews stands what is, by the writer's own admission, a "long and involved message" (5:11). This portion of his sermon, more than any other, has the potential to overwhelm twenty-first-century Christian readers who are admittedly far less familiar with the Old Testament than the preacher and his congregation. The preacher opens a window here into just how important the Old Testament was for the formation of Christian theology, even as he sets aside the old *covenant* that was laid down for Israel in the pages of the Old Testament in favor of the new covenant Jesus inaugurated.

The essence of the preacher's message to his congregation, however, is straightforward. They enjoy the great gift of being connected with a mediator—Jesus, the Son of God—who is in a better position to advance the relationship between God and human beings than any other mediator in history (7:1–8:6). This mediator, by willingly laying down his own life precisely in order to bring us such great gifts, has inaugurated the new covenant that God promised (as articulated through the prophet Jeremiah). Jesus has done what was necessary to accomplish the covenant's promises (the decisive removal of sin from our consciences and from God's memory). And he has made it possible at last for God's people to cross formerly impassable boundaries in their approach to God (that is, entry in

God's full presence in the eternal realm; 8:7–10:18). In light of all this, it only makes sense for Christians to hold onto their connection with this mediator at all costs, to keep openly celebrating this connection in their public witness and their life together, and to keep moving forward into that better future for which he fitted them at the cost of his very life (10:19-25).

A Better Mediator

The concept of a mediator was common, even universal, in the preacher's world. If a person needed help and identified someone who *could* help but was not in her immediate circle, she would look for someone who *was* in her circle who was also connected with the other person, who could go to that person on her behalf. We saw a centurion do this very thing as he strategized about how to get Jesus, a Galilean Jewish wonder worker, to heal his slave (Luke 7:1-10). He approached the Jewish residents of Capernaum, asking them to use their influence with their fellow Jew, Jesus! They were only too happy to do this, of course, since the centurion was a great benefactor of their village, and they probably did not have many opportunities to return his significant favor. Mediators were even more critically important where some junior party had previously offended a senior party and now found himself or herself in need of help from that senior party.

All of these dynamics were readily transferrable to the relationship between human beings and God or the gods, which explains the importance of priests in both Jewish and Greco-Roman religion. Priests were the people who knew how to approach deity in proper ways, so as to repair the relationship between humans and God or the gods and also secure favor and help from the divine.

The author of Hebrews has been comparing Jesus with other mediators since the beginning of his sermon. By the first century, angels were popularly thought of as one group of mediators between human beings and God. As Jews pictured God's space more and more as a heavenly temple, angels took on the roles of priests in that temple, bringing the prayers of human beings before God and bringing back God's answers, sometimes being dispatched to directly intervene.[1] The fact that Jesus has greater dignity than the angels, a dignity that comes from his occupying a position closer to God in God's household as the Son, already implies that Jesus is a more valuable mediator with whom to be connected.

Moses was long celebrated as a mediator and intercessor on Israel's behalf. He famously threw himself between God's anger and the ancient Hebrews on several occasions, most dramatically in the incident of the Golden Calf (Exodus 32:7-14, 30-34). One Jewish writer from around the turn of the era asserted that the memory of Moses's faithfulness and intercession continued to have an impact on God's relationship with the people of Israel. God declares that he will keep Moses's staff, the rod with which he performed God's signs in Egypt and in the desert, ever before him. When the people sin against God again, God will remember Moses and spare them. It would be a perpetual sign to God like Noah's rainbow.[2] The preacher has only good things to say about Moses, who was "faithful in God's house as a servant" (Numbers 12:7; Hebrews 3:5), but better things to say about Jesus, who is faithful "over God's house as a Son" (Hebrews 3:6). Once again, Jesus's superior placement in God's household signals Jesus's superior ability to connect those who seek God's favor through him with the help they need.

Continuing the "long and involved message," the preacher moves on to the more routine mediators between human beings and the one true God known from scripture and from practices within the Jerusalem temple: the priests descended from Levi. Levi was the third of the twelve sons of Jacob, and it fell to the lot of his descendants to attend to the work first of the tabernacle and then, in the reign of Solomon and beyond, of the temple. Their selection was also connected to the incident of the Golden Calf. When Moses confronted the Hebrews in the midst of their return to idolatry and asked, "Who is on the Lord's side?" it was the men of the tribe of Levi who came out to stand by him (Exodus 32:25-26). Moses commissioned them to carry out his sentence upon the Hebrews, killing a representative three thousand people among them. By doing this they consecrated themselves to the Lord's service (32:27-29). Henceforth, God and the holy things of God would be the tribe's inheritance among Israel.

Accepting the Levitical priests as a legitimate group of mediators, the preacher gives a great deal of attention to how Jesus is a better mediator, a better go-between connecting human beings and God. We have already seen how the preacher finds warrant in the Old Testament for believing that Jesus was indeed set apart by God to serve in this capacity. Just as the earliest followers of Jesus saw his life, death, and resurrection reflected in the psalms and Prophets, so they discovered indications of Jesus's ongoing career in those sacred texts. Clouds removed the ascending Jesus from the sight of his apostolic witnesses (Acts 1:1-11), but the sacred texts revealed what happened on the far side of those clouds and would yet happen in the future:

> The Lord said to my Lord, "Sit at my right hand until I set
> your enemies as a footstool under your feet."
> (Psalm 110:1; Hebrews 1:13)

God continues to speak in this same psalm, however, appointing the psalmist's "Lord" to the priesthood:

> The Lord has sworn and will not change his mind: "You
> are a priest forever in the line of Melchizedek."
> (Psalm 110:4; Hebrews 5:6, 10; 6:20; 7:17, 21).

Melchizedek does not get a lot of airtime in the Old Testament. He has a single cameo, appearing on the scene once as the "king of Salem" who was also "a priest of God Most High" (Genesis 14:17-20). It stuck in Israel's memory, however, that there was at one time a priest of the One God who was not descended from Levi, but rather predated his birth. Thus, Israel's kings could claim in Melchizedek some precedent for their own participation in the ritual life of the temple, despite not being Levites themselves.[3]

This obscure figure emerges as the founder of a priestly line that will be more distinguished and more effective than the priests descended from Levi and Aaron, the only other mediators sanctioned by scripture to facilitate interaction with God. Appointed as the second and last incumbent in the priestly line of Melchizedek, Jesus has a ministry "more excellent" than the Levitical priesthood because:

- Jesus is a priest whose everlasting ministry is guaranteed by God's oath: "The Lord has sworn, and will not change his mind" (7:20-21; Psalm 110:4).

- Jesus is a priest who "lives forever" to appeal to God on our behalf, to deliver completely those who draw near to God through him (7:25), unlike mortal priests, whose role will end with their deaths.

- Jesus is a priest with no relational blockages between himself and God, no sins for which he must first make amends before interceding on our behalf (7:27).

- Jesus is a priest who serves in a better sanctuary (8:2-5; 9:11-12, 24), in God's full presence, "more highly exalted in the heavens" (7:26).

This last point is especially important for the preacher, who shares with other Jews of the period the conviction that the tabernacle and Jerusalem temple were merely models or copies of God's throne room in heaven itself. These Jews read God's words to Moses in Exodus 25:40 as an indication that God revealed the heavenly temple to Moses when Moses was on Mount Sinai, telling Moses to make the tabernacle in imitation of the heavenly reality.[4] Mediation that could be carried out in the "real thing" was obviously better than mediation carried out in the "earthly copy."

Ultimately, however, Jesus's ministry is more excellent because it is more effective. Jesus offers a once-for-all sacrifice that achieves what countless repetitions of animal sacrifices could not (10:1-14). This achievement stands at the heart of the author's identification of God's new arrangements with the Christian community as a better covenant, the new covenant.

"Perfection"

To speak at all of a "new covenant" raises the question: What was wrong with the old covenant? The preacher senses this, as he presents Jeremiah 31:31-34 as evidence that God did, in fact, regard the first covenant as deficient. The prophet cites Israel's failure to continue faithfully in the covenant—their disobedience and, thus, their breaking of the covenant—as the cause for God setting it aside in favor of the new covenant (Jeremiah 31:31; Hebrews 8:7-9). But the deficiencies of the former covenant go beyond this for the preacher:

> If "perfection" had been attainable through the Levitical priesthood (for the people were regulated by the Torah on the basis of this priesthood), what need would there still be to speak of another priest who would rise up in the line of Melchizedek and not in the line of Aaron? (Hebrews 7:11)

> There is a setting aside of the earlier commandment on account of its weakness and ineffectiveness—for the Law "perfected" nothing—and the introduction of a better hope, through which we draw nearer to God. (7:18)

> The Law, bearing the shadow of the good things that were on the horizon but not the exact image of those things, is never able by the same sacrifices that they offer endlessly year after year to perfect those who are drawing near. (10:1)

The root of the problem with the old covenant was its inability to "perfect" the people.

Words related to *perfection* appear frequently in English translations of the Book of Hebrews.[5] This term, however, has connotations in English that the corresponding Greek family of words lacks. For example, there is no sense in Greek that perfection means doing everything correctly all the time or lining up flawlessly with an elevated standard. In other words, there is nothing of "perfectionism" in perfection here. Rather, the Greek words translated as "perfection" or related terms tend to speak of something arriving at its ultimate goal or being fully realized. Thus for the child, "perfection" means to become a full-fledged adult. (The word "mature" in the NRSV and CEB translations of Hebrews 5:14 reflects the same Greek root as the other words rendered "perfect" in English). Regarding a wish or purpose, perfection means that the intended action is accomplished or brought to pass. For a person seeking to join a mystery cult or secret society, perfection means that the would-be initiate has become a fully inducted member. For someone moving toward the priesthood, perfection means to arrive at the completion of the ordination process and rites. For the child of God, perfection means to be gathered into God's everlasting house and homeland.

At least, that seems to be the preacher's understanding of the idea, both from what he asserts did not happen under the Levitical priests and the covenant they upheld and what he affirms has been accomplished by Jesus, the priest in Melchizedek's line (and, as it happens, the sacrifice as well). The preacher looked upon the rigid barriers and restrictions on access to God under the old covenant as an arch-failing. The very architecture of the tabernacle and the temple proclaimed these restrictions. The Israelites from eleven tribes were barred from entering the sanctuary itself, having to content themselves with worshipping in the court of Israelite males and the court of women. The priests from the tribe of Levi, of the line of Aaron, were permitted to enter only the first room of the sanctuary (the "holy place"). The high priest alone was permitted to enter the inner room of the sanctuary (the "Holy of Holies"), and that only one day out of the year (Hebrews 9:1-10). None of the sacrifices performed by these priests were ever able to broaden access to God even in that earthly model of God's realm. Their very repetition was the proof of their ineffectiveness (10:1-4).

The preacher is convinced that the arrangements in place under the covenant of Moses, which were still in place more than a thousand years later during the ministry of Jesus and for several decades after his resurrection, were not achieving God's goal for human beings, which was to fit them to stand once again in God's full presence as they once had in Eden. These arrangements have value for the preacher, but only symbolic value. By means of them, "the Holy Spirit shows that the way into the Holy of Holies is not apparent as long as the first tent is standing, which is a figure for the present time" (9:8-9). The preacher alludes here to his expectations for the future, when God will shake and remove the visible earth and sky (the cosmic "outer tent") so that the way into the "unshakable kingdom" is made clear and evident (12:26-28). That "unshakable kingdom" is also God's eternal realm, the heavenly "holy of holies" of which the tabernacle and temple had been mere models.

God had prescribed a process by which Jesus would be qualified to act as "a merciful and faithful high priest" (2:17), a process that had involved his immersion into the challenges and hardships that the "many sons and daughters" who would be born into God's family through faith would face. Jesus was "perfected" (2:10; 5:9; 7:28) as he underwent the process of suffering, death, and exaltation that brought him to his final state: installation as an effective high priest in heaven.

> Christ emerged through the greater and more perfect tent—the one not made by hands—as high priest of the good things to come. (9:11)

> Christ did not enter into holy places fashioned by mortal hands—the copies of the genuine ones—but into heaven itself, now to appear before the face of God on our behalf. (9:24)

It is precisely for entrance into the same holy places—the full presence of God in God's eternal realm—that Jesus has fitted his followers by means of his sacrifice and priestly mediation:

> We therefore have boldness, brothers and sisters, to enter the holy places by the blood of Jesus through the new and life-giving path he inaugurated for us through the curtain (that is, through his flesh). (Hebrews 10:19-20)

We are "perfected" as we are cleansed and consecrated by Jesus for entrance into God's presence and as we move across that ultimate boundary beyond death or beyond the dissolution of the old creation. This is the perfection that the Levitical priests could not begin to make available but which the "better mediator" now offers to all who persevere in drawing close to God through him. The preacher wants his hearers to understand the value of having such a high priest who, by the offering of himself once for all, advanced the relationship between human beings and God far beyond what the priests in the Jerusalem temple, the priests in the line of Levi, had been able to achieve. With such unprecedented prospects before them, how could they contemplate breaking faith with the mediator who offers these provisions?

The language of "perfection" in Hebrews opens us up to the dynamic and the direction of discipleship. This is a connection generally muted in our English translations, since the language of "maturity" and the language of "perfection" reflect one common root in the Greek. The preacher calls us to "move ourselves forward to maturity," toward the completion of the journey of transformation begun in our baptism and in the laying of the foundation of Christian instruction (6:1). John Wesley would no doubt have found in the preacher of Hebrews a kindred spirit given his own emphasis on "Christian perfection," the maturity reflected in arriving at the freedom from the compulsion to sin and the freedom for living for Christ (or, better, finding Christ living in and through oneself).[6] But as we press on toward "maturity" in Christ (Hebrews 6:1), we also move forward in the direction of, and finally across, that ultimate threshold between the visible and the heavenly realm, toward our final goal (and thus perfection).

The Blood of the New Covenant

Readers of scripture know that, within the framework of the old covenant (the Law of Moses), only people descended from Levi could legitimately serve as priestly mediators. Within that framework, Jesus, who was descended from Judah, had no place serving as a priest, as the preacher freely admits (Hebrews 7:14; 8:4). This is why the preacher can and must say that "with a change in the priesthood, there is necessarily also a change in the law" (Hebrews 7:12). The old covenant and the Levitical priesthood were entirely interconnected and interdependent. The covenant established the priesthood; the priesthood repaired and maintained the covenant. God's appointment of Jesus as priest in the line of Melchizedek thus also signals God's setting aside of the old covenant and introduction of a new arrangement between God and God's people: the "new covenant" announced by Jeremiah (Jeremiah 31:31-34; Hebrews 8:8-12).

The preacher says of Jesus, our high priest, that "he has now received a ministry that is more distinguished [than the Levitical priesthood] to the degree that he is the mediator of a better covenant, which is set down on the basis of better promises" (8:6). He then recites the key text from Jeremiah, spoken in the same voice of God that had once spoken at Sinai and thus carrying the authority necessary to rescind and institute covenants:

> "Look! The days are coming," says the Lord,
> > "when I will put a new covenant into effect over the
> > house of Israel and the house of Judah.
> It will not be like the covenant that I made with their ancestors
> > on the day I took them by their hand to lead them out
> > from the land of Egypt,

because they did not continue in my covenant,
>   and I ceased to have a care for them," says the Lord.
"Because this is the covenant that I will make with the
house of Israel
>   after those days," says the Lord:
"Planting my laws in their mind,
>   I will write them upon their hearts
and I will be God to them,
>   and they will be a people for me
and a person will never again teach his or her fellow citizen
>   nor anyone a brother or sister, saying, 'Know the Lord!'
for they will all know me,
>   from the least to the greatest of them,
because I will be merciful in regard to their misdeeds
>   and will surely no longer hold their sins in memory."
>   (Jeremiah 31:31-34; Hebrews 8:8-12)

The "better promises" made in connection with this new covenant announce the decisive removal of the memory and the effects of sins committed and even the removal of the "bent toward sinning" that spawns new affronts to the holiness and majesty of God. The new covenant includes the provision for an obedience born and impelled from within (compare Romans 6:17-20). Anyone connected with Paul's mission would surely identify this as the result of the gift of the Holy Spirit (see, for example, Galatians 5:16-25; Romans 8:3-14). God thus announces the decisive removal of all that necessitated the carefully regulated and restricted access to God as modeled under the old covenant in the tabernacle and the temple, making possible the perfection of which the preacher speaks. We are now fit to enter God's eternal realm.

At this point, the preacher engages in a bold interpretation of the significance of a man's crucifixion for the rest of humankind. Of course, this particular crucifixion has significance only because of the man who suffered it and because God raised Jesus from the dead and received him into heaven itself in his ascension, an event the preacher holds frequently before his hearers (Hebrews 1:3, 6, 13; 4:14; 6:19-20; 8:1-2; 9:11, 24).[7] In order to give expression to the significance of Jesus's death, resurrection, and ascension for us, the preacher turns to the Old Testament for a framework of meaning. For him, "the law possessed the shadow of the good things that were coming" (10:1) and was, as such, instructive for unpacking the significance of those good things when they finally came about. Once again, this is a reminder to us that the Old Testament is indispensable for the Christian task of discerning the height and breadth and depth of the significance of Jesus's person and work.

In particular, the preacher looks to the Day of Atonement rites prescribed in Leviticus 16 and the covenant inauguration ceremony performed by Moses in Exodus 24:1-8. Leviticus 16 institutes a complex annual ritual to repair breaches to the covenant and dispel the destructive power of the pollution that had built up over a year from the people's sins. In the thinking of the ancient Israelite and the first-century Jew alike, the pollution of sin does not mix well with holiness. We should not think of oil and water here, which naturally separate, but of matter and anti-matter, which annihilate in a violent release of energy. The pollution of sin and defilement had to be kept below critical levels, as it were, if the holy God was to remain with the people and not lash out against the people to consume them. The Day of Atonement was a time for removing this pollution from among the people.

On the Day of Atonement, the high priest would sacrifice a bull to cleanse himself and his household from their sins. He would then take two goats. Laying his hands upon one of these goats, the high priest would recite the sins of the people and transfer them upon the head of the goat. This goat would then be driven off into the desert, carrying away the sins of the people. The high priest would sacrifice the second goat and carry some of its blood into the sanctuary to cleanse the Holy of Holies, the place representative of God's presence, from the pollution of the people's sin by sprinkling blood on the mercy seat and the altar. The carcasses of the bull and the goat would finally be taken outside the camp and burned.

The other ritual referenced by the writer of Hebrews, the covenant inauguration ritual of Exodus 24, was relatively simple by comparison. Moses read the book of the covenant, the people agreed to the terms, and Moses took the blood of a number of bulls, pouring some out at the base of the altar and spattering the people with the rest. The preacher goes a bit beyond this to say that Moses also sprinkled the tabernacle and the sacred vessels (Hebrews 9:19-22).

The preacher sees in these rituals the template for and keys to what Jesus achieved on our behalf. First, Jesus's death and ascension effect a cosmic Day of Atonement. Jesus can bypass making any offering for himself, as he, unlike the high priests in Aaron's line, had not sinned against God and needed to make no reparations (Hebrews 7:27). Jesus "suffered outside the camp in order to sanctify the people through his blood" (Hebrews 13:12), just as the sin-bearing goat was sent outside the camp and the bodies of the sin offerings were disposed of outside the camp. Jesus also went into the holy places—not those of the humanly made temple in Jerusalem, but those of the divinely made cosmic temple in God's realm—"now to appear before the face of God on our behalf" (Hebrews 9:24), cleansing the heavenly Holy of Holies not with physical blood, but with the testimony of his perfect obedience that involved his pouring out of his blood "outside the camp." The "better promises" of the new covenant are thus brought to pass. Just as the blood of the bulls and goats was sprinkled on the people to inaugurate the first covenant, our participation in the death of Jesus by our baptism applies his obedient death to our hearts, fitting us to enter God's presence "with our hearts sprinkled clean from a stained conscience" (Hebrews 10:22). Just as the Holy of Holies in the Jerusalem temple was cleansed with the blood of bulls and goats, so the defiling evidence of sin is removed from God's presence by Jesus's presence in the heavenly realm.

These two acts mirror the covenant inauguration ceremony,

this time inaugurating the new covenant. The connection between Jesus's death and the inauguration of the new covenant was well-established throughout the Christian churches wherever Christians gathered around the bread and the cup (see 1 Corinthians 11:23-26). The preacher's genius lay in taking the further step of exploring how the promises associated with the new covenant (in Jeremiah 31:33-34) became reality in the offering of the same body and blood on Calvary's cross.

The Problem of a Human Sacrifice

How can early Christians look to the execution of a human being and see an atoning sacrifice? Indeed, where did God ever authorize such an unconventional sacrifice? We can look to Leviticus and read prescriptions, ostensibly given by God, for animal sacrifices based on the principle that "a creature's life is in the blood. [God has] provided you the blood to make reconciliation for your lives on the altar, because the blood reconciles by means of the life" (Leviticus 17:11 CEB). When did the blood of bulls and goats lose their cleansing power as the preacher rather stunningly claims (Hebrews 10:4)? On the one hand, the very repetition of animal sacrifices year after year after year—and the absence of any change in who had how much access to God in the temple—said something to the preacher about the lack of real power in *that* blood (Hebrews 10:1-3). On the other hand, the astoundingly fresh and powerful experience of the Spirit of the living God in the midst of the Christian community said something to the preacher about the decisive change that happened in the human-divine relationship as a consequence of Jesus's death.

The preacher once again discovers the explanation in the Old Testament Scriptures, this time by reading Psalm 40:6-8 and imagining Jesus as the speaker:

You did not desire a sacrifice or offering,
but you prepared a body for me.
You were not pleased with burnt offering or sin offering.
Then I said: "Look! I have come to do your will, O God"
(as it is written about me in a chapter of the scroll).

(Psalm 40:6-8; Hebrews 10:5-7)

Several of the Hebrew prophets criticize the leaders and people of Israel and Judah for thinking that their many animal sacrifices keep God satisfied, when they ought to have offered their obedience instead in the first place (see, for example, Isaiah 1:11-13, 16-17; Jeremiah 7:21-23; Hosea 6:6; Amos 5:21-24). This was also surely the point of the original psalm, that God prefers for the worshipper to present himself or herself for obedience ("I have come to do your will") rather than to make up for disobedience with the blood of bulls and goats. The preacher, however, reads the psalm in light of the incarnation of the Son. The body, born of Mary, was prepared for the Son by God to serve as a better sacrifice than "burnt offering[s] and sin offering[s]" offered under the old covenant: "By God's will we have been consecrated through the single, decisive offering of the body of Jesus Christ" (Hebrews 10:10).

Obedience, of course, still remains the key ingredient in this sacrifice. It is not the fact that Jesus died that produced such benefits for humankind but the fact that Jesus died as a result of his steadfast commitment to obey God to the uttermost and to the end. As the preacher's co-worker Paul would write elsewhere, "just as the many were made sinners through the disobedience of the one person," namely Adam, "in the same way the many were made righteous through the obedience of the one man," Jesus Christ (Romans 5:19).

There was some precedent for this way of thinking in the century or so leading up to Jesus's birth. Beginning in about 175 BC, the leaders of the Jewish people departed in some striking ways from the covenant, setting aside the law of Moses as the political constitution of the state and adopting a Greek constitution and its related institutions instead. The disasters that befell Judea in the years that followed were later understood as God's punishment for the disloyalty of a sizable portion of its elite and their circles. When the Jews' continued observance even of the apolitical regulations of the Law of Moses came under attack, a number of Jews refused to abandon covenant loyalty. After their arrest, they endured being tortured to death rather than eat a mouthful of pork as a sign of their willingness to leave the old ways behind. Reflecting on their steadfast obedience unto death, later writers came to believe that their acts of covenant loyalty had value not only for the righteous martyrs themselves, but also for the disobedient nation. The author of 2 Maccabees writes that "the Lord's anger had turned to mercy" in answer to the martyrs' prayers (7:37-38; 8:5), with the result that God delivered the faithful Jews from both the apostate leaders and the foreign overlords through the Maccabean Revolt. The author of 4 Maccabees, reflecting on the same story, spoke of the martyrs' deaths in even more overtly sacrificial terms: "they became, as it were, a ransom for the nation's sins, and through the blood of those godly people and through the propitiatory offering of their deaths, divine providence saved Israel after it had been mistreated" (17:21-22).

Similar thinking undergirds Paul's and the preacher's view of the death of Jesus, the righteous one who "humbled himself, becoming obedient unto death, even the death of the cross" (Philippians 2:8). The death of Jesus, however, presents a more complicated scenario, for in Jesus we do not merely find a man offering perfect obedience to God in order to change God's relationship to sinners for the better; we find God offering himself to humankind so as to change human beings' hearts toward God for the better as well. It is not sufficient to see, upon the cross, Jesus offering himself to an angry God to bear the punishment deserved by others. One must also see God offering God's own self to ungrateful and rebellious human beings, seeking to win back his own creatures by a second astounding act of selfless generosity. These dynamics combine to make Jesus a better mediator in every way.

Continuing in the (New) Covenant

Jeremiah attributes the failure of the first covenant to the ancient Hebrews not heeding their obligations under the old covenant: "they did not continue in my covenant, and I ceased to be concerned about them" (Hebrews 8:9; Jeremiah 31:32). Not continuing to walk in line with the covenant led to the withdrawal of God's care and benefits. This action had its corollary under the new covenant as well, when Jeremiah speaks of God's commandments being written on the minds and hearts of God's people precisely so that they can and will obey, will follow through on their side of the covenant, and will continue to enjoy the covenant relationship with God and all God's blessings (Hebrews 8:10; Jeremiah 31:33). A deeper obedience is enabled, and is therefore expected, under this new covenant.

Continuing "in God's covenant" is precisely what was at stake for some members of the congregation, who were finding the pressures of their neighbors too much to bear in the long run and who were faltering in their hope for God's future benefits (see 2:1-4; 3:12-14; 4:1, 11; 6:4-8; 10:26-31; 12:16-17). The superior value of this covenant, its promises, and the mediator who inaugurated it gives Christ-followers far greater cause to continue. These covenant obligations are more relationally conceived, rather than spelled out in all the details as in the Law of Moses. In effect, Christians are called to show the Son of God his due as a benefactor who has bestowed the greatest of gifts at the greatest cost to himself. Christians are called, quite simply, to "show gratitude" (12:28), seeking to please God in all situations. Showing gratitude calls for obedience to Jesus (5:9), which includes following his example (12:2-3). It calls for staying loyal to God, to Jesus, and to the community of faith, whatever the cost in terms of worldly pleasures or hardships (for example, the experiences of 10:32-34; 13:3). It means always acting in the way that will honor God and the name of Jesus, rather than treating them and their gifts with contempt and bringing the name into disrepute

(6:4-8; 10:26-31). It means taking up our duties as people who have been given the great honor of being consecrated to God's service.

This is the implication of the preacher's language when he speaks of Jesus having made his followers "clean" specifically "to go about serving the living God" (Hebrews 9:14). This is the language of priestly service, though the preacher falls short of calling the hearers "priests" themselves, no doubt because he has just dismantled the system of regulated and restricted access to God in the temple system that relied on a class of priests to serve on behalf of the lay Israelites. He will go on to urge his hearers to keep offering to God the sacrifices that God finds acceptable: "Through Jesus Christ, let us always offer to God the sacrifice of praise—the fruit of lips that profess God's name. Let us not forget to do good and to share, for God is well pleased with sacrifices of this kind" (13:15-16). The call to such (priestly) service is the call to keep claiming God and Jesus in the face of their unsupportive neighbors, continuing to extend God's invitation to them as well to receive all that the Son has made available to his loyal clients, and to keep putting themselves out to support and encourage their fellow Christians who come more directly under fire than themselves.

The preacher does not lose sight of the forward-looking dimension of our deliverance or Jesus's acts on our behalf. Just as the people eagerly waited for the high priest to emerge from the holy places and return to them, assuring them of God's reaffirmation of favor toward the penitent people, so Christ's followers eagerly await the return of *their* great high priest from the heavenly Holy of Holies to complete their deliverance (Hebrews 9:28). Continuing in the covenant is not only necessary as a response of gratitude; it is also necessary as a means of arriving at the good end that God has prepared for us and we have yet to enter. And there remain yet two ways to encounter the Son at his return: as his loyal and obedient beneficiaries "who eagerly await him" or as the enemies whose subjugation at his return is assured (9:28; 10:13).

Five

Faithful Response in Action

(Hebrews 10:19–11:40)

People are willing to invest a great deal, expend significant effort, and endure substantial hardship in order to hold onto relationships or pursue goals they value highly. Throughout Hebrews, and particularly within the dense core of 7:1–10:18, the preacher seeks to help his hearers remember the value of their connection with Jesus—the Son of God—and the outcome he has prepared for them. Now he urges them to move forward in a manner that shows they do, in fact, place the appropriate value on this connection and outcome, lest they find themselves making choices that reflect too slight regard for the one seated at God's right hand. With the gift of the knowledge of the truth about God and God's Messiah comes the awesome responsibility of living in light of that truth.

If faith indeed saves us, what is the nature of that faith? This is precisely the focus of the celebrated "faith chapter," Hebrews 11, the most well-known and beloved chapter of the book. The faith that leads to "the preservation of our souls" (10:39) is not merely an assent to some propositions about a crucifixion and its effects. It is an orientation to God that takes action, sometimes drastically changing the direction of one's life in light of God's promises or warnings. It is a commitment embodied in decision after decision to choose the path that meets with God's approval irrespective of the response of human beings, especially of those who do not yet know God. It is a determination to move forward in obedience to God in the conviction that honoring God is the highest value and priority after having experienced God's loving kindness. It is to such a response of grateful loyalty—of faith—to which the preacher calls his hearers in every time, as long as it is called "today."

There's a Right Way to Respond to These Gifts . . .

The preacher transitions from his "long and involved message" to his exhortation (the "what now?") by summarizing the principal advantages that his hearers have gained and the cost incurred by Jesus to secure these advantages for them. Their relationship with and access to God have developed to an unprecedented level. While under the old covenant people relied on fallible human priests to restore them to God's good graces and secure God's favor, they now have "a great high priest" who, as Son, is set "over God's house" at God's right hand (10:21). Under the old covenant one Israelite was authorized to enter the earthly model of God's throne room once a year, but they have now been given confident assurance of their right to enter God's eternal realm into the unmasked and unmediated presence of God forever (10:19-20). They have been cleansed inside and out by the water of baptism, which washed their bodies, and the sacrifice of Jesus, which purified their consciences (10:22). And let us not forget what lies behind the pressing need to be granted such right of entry: the temporary nature of the created realm, which offers no eternally safe haven (1:10-12; 12:26-29). Even if some have doubts about the cataclysmic ending that the preacher, like other early Christian teachers, anticipated for the material creation, they cannot doubt the certainty of the decisive end awaiting them individually.

Taken just on their own, gifts of such value demand a grateful response to match, one that displays a clear understanding of the value of the gifts and acts in line with that understanding. But the personal *investment* of the one who secured gifts is also a significant part of this equation. The preacher keeps the cost of securing these gifts front and center here as he speaks of Jesus paving the way into the heavenly holy place for us "through his own flesh" and giving us the boldness to enter "by his own blood" (Hebrews 10:19-20). Such *investment* in the relationship calls for investment to match from the recipient and, while the preacher's hearers may have indeed invested a great deal in terms of accepting the loss of their personal property and security, they "have not yet resisted to the point of blood" (12:4) as Jesus had.

In light of all of this, what is the right way forward? The preacher lays out a direction with three complementary exhortations:

- "Let's keeping drawing closer with a sincere heart in the full assurance that comes from trusting, having sprinkled our hearts clean from the remembrance of wickedness and having washed our bodies with pure water."
- "Let's hold fast to the profession of our hope unwaveringly, because the One who promised is reliable."
- "And let's keep a close eye on one another so that love and good works burst forth as a result, not forsaking our meeting together, as is the habit of some, but encouraging one another—and let us do so all the more as we see the Day drawing closer!" (Hebrews 10:22-25)

He urges his hearers to "keep drawing closer" to the threshold between this world and the next, between the visible creation and the eternal realm they've been fitted to enter. In their present situation, of course, this does not call for physical movement across space. It calls for the continued movement of their attachments and their yearnings toward the life into which God has called them, toward the person the Spirit is shaping them to become, and toward ever more complete commitment to the Son who is rescuing them. It also calls for persevering in a move across social spaces. "Drawing closer" to the threshold of God's presence means drawing closer to one another in the space of Christian worship in which God's presence is experienced as a foretaste of eternity and God's help is found for persevering in loyalty to the Christian group and the distinctive witness of Christian life and practice (see also 4:14-16). Drawing closer—moving forward—calls for commitment to leaving a great deal behind as well, rather than yielding to the impulses to return.

The preacher also urges his hearers to "hold fast to the profession of our hope unwaveringly." The word translated "profession" here can have either or both of two senses. On the one hand, it can speak of internal assent or agreement, something like, "Let's hold on internally to what the Christian gospel tells us about the hope that lies before us." On the other hand, it can speak of public affirmation or profession, as in, "Let's not back down from our public ownership of and alignment with the hope that lies before us." If pressed for clarity, the preacher would be hard put to make a choice between the two meanings since he has spent a great deal of time assuring his congregation of the reliability of their hope (the internal facet) and equal time spurring them on to maintain the public face of their faith even in the midst of serious pressure to the contrary.

Once again, the preacher stresses the vital importance of social support within the Christian community to sustain commitment in the face of those pressures. The NRSV translates Hebrews 10:24 as "let us consider how to provoke one another to love and good deeds." The CEB's translation is similar: "let us consider each other carefully for the purpose of sparking love and good deeds." The Greek here is a bit more ambiguous. A more transparent rendering would be: "Let us look closely at one another, leading to an outburst/stimulation of love and good deeds." The NRSV and CEB understand the preacher to be encouraging us to consider *how* to get *each other* to show greater love and invest more in doing good. The preacher, however, may well be encouraging his hearers to look more closely and purposefully at their sisters and brothers in Christ and at their circumstances and needs with a view to investing *themselves* in showing greater love and lending support.[1] Such an exhortation is particularly necessary in light of the fact that some of these believers have already begun "shrinking back" (10:39) rather than "drawing closer," ceasing to attend Christian worship meetings. Their goal is, of course, to relieve themselves of their neighbors' suspicion, disapproval, and pressure. But watching one's sisters and brothers withdraw cannot help but have an erosive effect on one's own commitment as well, stimulating such thoughts as, "If Aristion and Isidora don't think this is all worth it any more, why do I still?" Perseverance requires precisely the opposite dynamic within the Christian group.

The first example of faithful response that the preacher holds up before the members of this Christian community is their own past conduct:

> Remember the earlier days, during which you endured a great contest of sufferings, in part being made a public spectacle through reproaches and afflictions, in part making yourselves partners with those who were being thus treated. For you expressed sympathy for those in prison and welcomed the seizure of your property with joy, since you knew yourselves to have better and lasting possessions.
>
> (10:32-34)

Honor, or being viewed as a worthy part of the social group by one's peers, was a primary value in the first-century Mediterranean region. Honor was precisely the point at which peers hit the Christian converts the hardest, using a variety of shaming techniques to pressure them into returning to the values and practices the larger society embraced. It was remarkable that they had persevered in the face of such pressure; it was even more remarkable that those who had not been singled out for direct shaming stood alongside those who had been, showing their solidarity with and support for them at the cost of painting targets on their own backs as well. Such was their conviction, their commitment to their common hope and to one another, and their boldness in the face of their neighbors' disapproval. To arrive at God's good goal for them and make good on their past sacrifices, they now simply needed to recover their former commitment: "Don't cast your boldness aside, for it holds a great reward. You have need of endurance now so that, having done what God's will required, you may receive what was promised!" (10:35-36).

Many readers will have to acknowledge the distance between our own experience and the experience of the Christians whom the preacher addresses. His exhortations still call us to move in healthful and necessary directions, for we, too, need to continually examine ourselves. Are our best investments of our time, energy, and resources directed toward the world that is, in some sense, *behind* us, or toward the kingdom of God that lies in front of us? Are we sufficiently assured of and boldly maintaining the hope that Christ has set before us? Do we pull together around those who are struggling or faltering, for whatever reason, in their commitment to keep moving forward toward fuller discipleship?

But the preacher's words address a different sector of the global Christian church much more directly. There are Christians in India, Sri Lanka, Nepal, Iraq, and Pakistan who can identify immediately with the pressures faced by the preacher's ancient audience, enduring verbal abuse, physical assaults, the loss or destruction of personal property, and even imprisonment. They have persevered in their commitment to Jesus and hold on to Christian hope in the face of all such onslaughts. There are Christians in North Korea, Eritrea, Nigeria, and South Sudan whose commitment has been far more severely tested and who have paid even more dearly than the preacher's ancient audience. Scriptures such as our sermon "to the Hebrews," which speak to these sisters and brothers so much more directly than to us, should serve to keep *us* mindful of *them* and of our obligation to them as part of our family in Christ. If we were to look intently at them, the challenges they face, and the sacrifices they make in order to "keep drawing near" to the God who calls them and the Lord who redeemed them, how might we be stimulated to respond with love and good works as vessels of the "timely help" they might even now be seeking from God's throne of favor (4:16)?[2]

. . .And a Wrong Way

Responding well, fully, and faithfully to God's generous gifts and promises in Christ is not optional. For the preacher, it is the *only* way forward. The path on which we all found ourselves prior to Christ's intervention in our lives would have ended in disaster. Paul attributed this disaster to humanity's fundamental failure to respond graciously to the God who bestowed on us the very gift of existence in a world well-suited to sustain us (Romans 1:18-23), choosing instead to abuse God's gift of life. But now to deliberately choose to return to that path rather than continue in loyalty toward Christ—after God's even more gracious provision for the redemption of and reconciliation with the rebellious creation—would heap insult upon insult against the majesty of God.

> For if we willfully continue to sin after receiving knowledge of the truth, there is no sacrifice for sin left to us but only a fearsome expectation of judgment and of a fire that is eager to devour God's adversaries.
>
> A person setting aside the law of Moses dies without mercy on the testimony of two or three people. Of how much worse punishment do you think the person who trampled the Son of God underfoot, considered ordinary the blood by which he or she had been sanctified, and insolently affronted the Spirit of grace will be deemed worthy? For we know the One who said:
>
> "Vengeance belongs to me; I will repay";

and again,

"The Lord will judge his people."

It is a fearsome thing to fall into the hands of the living God! (Hebrews 10:26-31)

The Law of Moses distinguished between sin committed without intent and "willful sin." In Numbers 15:22-31, the latter is called sinning "with a high hand" and is an act of arrogant rebellion against God by making a conscious decision not to give God the obedience that was God's due as the nation's deliverer and protector, choosing another path instead. For such sins, there was no provision for atonement, no sacrifice, under the old covenant. Given the decisive, unrepeatable, "once-for-all" nature of Jesus's giving of himself for us, the preacher claims that there is no further provision for atonement under the new covenant as well.

Given the situation his Christian hearers were facing, the preacher no doubt thought of "willful sin" here as drawing back from the Christian community, perhaps moving again in the religious spheres that would assure the (former) Christian's neighbors that he or she had returned to an acceptably pious lifestyle following the traditional gods. It is no accident that he will name the alternative to exhibiting "faith" as "shrinking back" (10:37-39). Indeed, the preacher has just referred to this quiet defection on the part of some (10:25) and seeks to head off any further defections by depicting the significance and consequences of such a course change as starkly as possible. Once again, he asks his hearers to consider the strictness with which the old covenant was enforced, referring specifically to the prescription of the death penalty for any Israelite discovered to have committed idolatry "on the testimony of two or three witnesses" (Deuteronomy 17:6; Hebrews 10:28). If God commanded such enforcement of a lesser covenant instituted through lesser mediators and maintained by lesser priests (the thrust of all the comparisons the preacher has made since the outset of the sermon), should the hearers imagine that God would respond less forcefully to violations of the covenant relationship inaugurated by God's Son?

The preacher asks them to consider what taking the path of least resistance in their situation really looks like from the perspective of this covenant relationship. Drawing back from the Christian fellowship and saying to their neighbors, in effect, "Your friendship and acceptance are more valuable to me than the friendship and favor God had offered me through Jesus," could indeed be nothing less than stomping on Jesus, showing contempt for the value of his blood, and outrageously meeting God's desire to extend favor with insult. In their situation, a choice must be made in regard to whom to alienate. The preacher is not shy in urging them not to choose to alienate God once again after God extended such a gracious invitation back into favor through God's Son. It was remarkable for God to show further grace to the ignorantly ungrateful. What should the willfully ungrateful expect?

The picture of God and the emotions the preacher evokes in regard to God in this paragraph are not popular in twenty-first-century Western Christianity. God is presented as one who holds people accountable for their actions and responses and who visits judgment upon those who have persisted in outrages against God's honor and the honor of the Son. The preacher promotes the fear of God—a deep respect for God's honor and an aversion to the consequences of abusing God's honor—as a good and healthy thing even for Christians to maintain. Many of us shy away from the notion as perhaps too primitive a view of God, yet our scriptural heritage promotes this understanding rather consistently. Jesus himself seems to have thought of God's patience as having limits and God's justice manifesting itself both in deliverance and vengeance (see, for example, Matthew 13:41-43; 25:31-46). Paul also noted "fear and trembling" as appropriate shades of religious emotion and motivation in light of the stakes involved in making the best and fullest use of the favor God had extended (Philippians 2:12-13). And he regarded God's "wrath" against injustice and unholiness as something from which people of faith still looked for deliverance, although with confidence (Romans 2:9-11; 5:9-10). The majority of New Testament voices would still concur with the ancient Israelite proverb: "Fearing the Lord is the beginning of wisdom," the starting point for making wise decisions and choices (Proverbs 9:10).

We are often intentionally mindful of the feelings and responses of others as we go about our daily lives and work. Sometimes we choose to take unpopular positions and invite significant opposition from one person or group because of our loyalty or attachments to another person. We are accustomed to weighing what is due to a friend, a co-worker, or a family member, and this process shapes our decisions about what course of action we will undertake. The preacher simply urges his hearers to do no less when it comes to God and to Jesus—to think of God not as an impersonal reservoir of grace but as a personal being who extends favor and looks for the fruits such favor ought to produce (6:7-8). God's favor is meant not only to "make us right" with God, but to move us to conduct ourselves rightly in our restored relationship with God. For the preacher, that means choosing to live day by day in ways that reflect our proper valuing of the relationship and the cost Jesus incurred (that is, the cost the Trinity absorbed) to restore it. Love for and gratitude to God should always be our primary motivations. But, as far as the preacher is concerned, when love and gratitude fail to provide sufficient motivation and, on the other hand, fear of God drives us in the direction that love and gratitude ought to have done, we are still moving forward toward deliverance.

While many Christians around the globe today have to wrestle with the same temptation to the particular sin that the preacher addressed in his hearers' immediate situation, his warning to leave sin behind has far wider applicability. Whenever we find ourselves tempted to return to the practices from which Christ died to redeem us, we are in danger of insulting Jesus, showing contempt for the value of his blood. Whenever we choose the rewards of suppressing our witness or of hiding our affiliation with Jesus, whenever we choose the temporary pleasure of a particular sinful practice, whenever we find ourselves investing far more in advancing our own interests in the world than in advancing God's, we find ourselves in danger of abusing God's grace. God intends for his favor to change the fundamental orientation of our lives so that our hearts and yearnings are centered on our Creator, as they should always have been. God's investment in us on the cross of Calvary was so dramatic, in part, to communicate to us the amplitude of the response we would have to make. In Paul's words, Christ "died for all so that those who continued living might not keep on living for themselves, but for him who died and was raised on their behalf" (2 Corinthians 5:15).[3] If we value the cost, we will better evaluate our responses, which will show God precisely how much or how little we value it.

Faith in Action

The section of Hebrews that may be the most familiar to the greatest number of readers is the celebrated "faith chapter." Here the preacher lists the great heroes of faith known from the Old Testament (and other early Jewish literature) and provides vignettes showing how their faith expressed itself in their choices and actions. The so-called faith chapter, however, is not something that is easily lifted from its context in the sermon or the immediate context the preacher was addressing. Although it speaks eloquently to Christians in every time and place concerning the nature of genuine faith in action, the preacher himself selected and shaped the various portraits of faith to speak quite pointedly to the challenges and choices facing his congregation. The author desired to supply examples of faithful decisions and actions to a congregation in hopes that they would "imitate those who through faith and perseverance inherited what was promised" (6:12).

The preacher begins his parade of the heroes of faith with a definition of faith (or trust) that, unfortunately, includes two words in the original Greek that are very difficult to define. Consider these translations of Hebrews 11:1:

> Now faith is the assurance [*hypostasis*] of things hoped for, the conviction [*elenchus*] of things not seen. (NRSV)

> Faith is the reality [*hypostasis*] of what we hope for, the proof [*elenchus*] of what we don't see. (CEB)

The NRSV focuses the definition on what our experience of trusting *feels* like: it *feels* like "assurance" and "conviction," confidence concerning the reception of good things in the future. The CEB tries to bring out, by contrast, the effect and significance of trusting, which essentially puts the things for which we hope in our possession, making them "reality," and gives "proof" to the world of the invisible realities that move us as effects always bear witness to causes.

The Greek word *hypostasis* (high-PAW-stuh-siss) is the more slippery of the two. In one sense, it can be used to speak of the "foundation" of a building or of some enterprise; it can also be used to speak about the origin of something else or the strategy by which something is brought about. Abraham and Sarah's trust in God's promise was the origin of Isaac and his whole line, for it was their trust that led them to try for a child one more time. The preacher may be urging his hearers to hold onto their trust in God (and thus continue to live in loyalty to God and God's Son) because such trust will lead to the good and eternal destiny that God promises them. Their trust will be like a seed is to the tree that it will become, or like a foundation is to the house that will one day take shape upon it.

The word *hypostasis* is also used in more mundane, commercial contexts in the preacher's world. For example, it is used to speak of a sum of money placed on deposit and even of title deeds to land. Abraham's trust in God's promise and his departure from his homeland at God's direction were, figuratively speaking, the deposit Abraham made on his future inheritance. In light of the preacher's declaration just a moment before that at least some members of his audience have allowed themselves to be deprived of their property because they knew that they had "better and lasting possessions" by virtue of their connection with Jesus (10:34), one might wonder whether he has such meanings in mind here: "Continuing in faith is your 'money down' on your better and lasting possessions," or even, "The trust you place and continue to place in God is your title deed to the better and lasting possessions that God has in store for you."

The Greek word *elenchus* (eh-LENG-kuss) was a common legal term meaning "evidence" or "proof." The kind of lifestyle and actions that trusting in God's promises and committing oneself to God's values produces becomes a *living witness to a greater reality.* A person's willingness to chart his or her course with a view to meeting with God's approval at Christ's return and entering God's eternal presence becomes a living witness to the destination itself. The ark that Noah constructed was a demonstration—the visible and tangible evidence—of the flood that was coming. Moses's decision to align himself with the Hebrews in their slavery, leaving behind the luxurious palaces of Pharaoh, was evidence that the God of the Hebrews was real, that being allied with God was more strategic and advantageous, and that God's rewards were greater and more lasting. People of faith make "visible" the invisible God and his promises, at least in the traces these leave in their lives. For this reason, people who live by faith can stimulate faith in us. In their response to the unseen, we "see" more of the reality of the unseen and grow in our conviction and our ability to invest our own lives in the direction in which faith leads.

Of course, we don't have to rely only on the meaning of these two Greek words. The way the writer describes faith in Hebrews 11 can give us a richer understanding of what he means. A number of threads run throughout the tapestry of faith that the preacher weaves. One is that *faith acts with a view to the unseen.* Trusting God requires looking beyond what is currently accessible through any of the five senses. Faith is not "blind," as if the person of faith closes his or her eyes to reality. Rather, people of faith have opened themselves up to larger dimensions of reality than the five senses can grasp. Indeed, only "by faith" can we fathom the many dimensions of reality and make wise choices and commitments, informed by the fuller truth of our existence as not only material but also spiritual beings. The words "by faith" run like a refrain throughout the chapter, introducing each new model of faith-in-action from Abel (11:4) through Rahab (11:31). The first occurrence of this refrain, however, introduces not an example of faith but a presupposition of faith: "By faith we understand the ages [or "the worlds"] to have been established by God's speaking, so that what is visible did not come into being from things we can observe" (11:3).

In a chapter that celebrates the heroes of faith, this statement may seem a bit cerebral. Nevertheless, it articulates a perspective that is essential if we are indeed to live by faith, a perspective that informs the examples of many of the heroes celebrated in this chapter. Everything that can be seen—the entire material universe—exists because God's word spoke it into existence. All that can be seen is dependent upon, and therefore secondary to, the word of God. Such thinking flies in the face of our materialist culture. I use the word *materialist* here not in the sense of our widespread addiction to shopping and consumerism (though this is a symptom). Rather, I use it in the sense of the widespread perception that only what can be experienced by the five senses is "real," or that this is, at least, the basic reality underlying our existence and experience. For the person of faith, however, the most real, the most solid, the most foundational thing is the word God speaks to that person. "Heaven and earth will pass away," but God's word and the word of God's Son endures forever, as will those who build their lives around that word (Matthew 7:24-27; 24:35).

Noah took action "after being warned about things not yet observable" (11:7). The word of the God who warned him was more real to Noah than his own meteorological savvy or his and his people's collective memory, in which there was no precedent for such a cataclysm. Moses steadfastly endured in the direction in which he set out—away from the palaces of Egypt, into the company of slaves, into confrontation with Pharaoh, through the Red Sea, through a lifetime of wandering in the desert—"as one who saw the Invisible" (11:27). Arriving at such a vivid perception of the invisible, however, requires significant intentionality and investment in the midst of a world that floods our senses (especially those of sight and sound) from waking to sleeping, distracting our attention from and dulling our perception of the invisible God and God's inaudible voice.

I have lived most of my life in cities or, at least, densely populated areas. There is always a haze of light around me when I step out into the night. I never realized how bright and plentiful the stars were until I attended a conference in Montana and stepped out to view the night sky. Similarly, many Christians throughout the centuries have valued and prioritized finding quiet places: places where any visual stimuli that do exist point them beyond temporary realities, places where the physical senses can retire, and where they can connect with God. For myself, the more time I spend in God's presence, in prayer, and in listening to God, the more the divine reality impresses itself upon me, the perspective of faith is restored, and the directions in which faith leads become evident.[4]

A second thread that runs throughout the examples in this chapter is that *faith acts with a view to the future*, more specifically, God's future. Walking by faith requires taking God's announcements about the future with utmost seriousness. Abraham could not stay comfortably at home in Haran where everyone knew his family and his good reputation if he was ever to become the vehicle through which nations would receive God's blessing, as God promised (11:8). Joseph showed how faith looks toward God's action even beyond one's own death, giving his children instructions about taking his bones up from Egypt into Canaan. These instructions were passed on to their children, and so on for generations, until the Exodus was accomplished over four centuries later (Hebrews 11:22; see Genesis 50:24-25).

Moses also persevered in his downwardly mobile career "because he was looking ahead to the reward" (11:26). Moses's faith is the opposite of such distrust as the wilderness generation displayed when they sought to return to Egypt rather than move confidently against the inhabitants of Canaan in obedience to God's command (Hebrews. 3:7-19). Because they did not regard God as a reliable benefactor, they failed to move forward as faith would have directed, and so provoked rather than pleased God. Trust in God's promises is essential for faithful discipleship. It is often only our belief in God's promised rewards that allows us to face difficult challenges—whether resisting temptations to sin, facing strong opposition while standing up for what is right, or investing ourselves in serving others and relieving their need rather than building up our own portfolios—and thus to please God (11:6).

But it is Noah who perhaps provides the most dramatic example of this kind of faith at work. Hearing God's message, Noah and his whole family dedicated themselves entirely to preparing for that future. We have no idea what Noah's original occupation was. All we know is that when God told him to prepare a gigantic lifeboat, he and his household set to work building a gigantic lifeboat. God's announcement concerning the future changed Noah's and his family's entire agenda for every day between that announcement and running aground on Mount Ararat. The entirely new orientation of his life and the new direction in which he put all his energies and resources to work (and not just his free time or his Sunday mornings!) were a living testimony to God and God's warning. It was the faith in action that gave visible proof to as-yet-unseen circumstances. The result of building a lifeboat in response to God's warning, however, was nothing less than "the deliverance of his household" (11:7).

In the same way, Jesus promises that building our lives afresh from the ground up on the foundation of his teachings will result in our own deliverance in the face of the cataclysms yet to come (Matthew 7:24-27). Noah appears with some regularity in the pages of the New Testament, since early Christians perceived a close analogy to exist between Noah's situation and theirs as they looked forward to God's forthcoming visitation (see Matthew 24:36-39; 1 Peter 3:20-21; 2 Peter 3:3-7). They proclaim with one voice: Christ is coming again for the deliverance of those who took his word with utmost seriousness rather than neglecting it or taking it lightly (Hebrews 2:1-2; 9:28) but for the indictment of those who persisted in dishonoring God by their disdain for righteousness (Hebrews 10:26-31). Faith lives ever with a view to standing approved on that day, whatever the price of faithful living today. Until a full week or more into the rains, Noah most likely was regarded as a complete idiot by his neighbors for building a huge boat in the middle of a landlocked plain. Perhaps Noah looked at his own behavior as foolish during the long, sunny stretches of the Mesopotamian summer. Committing ourselves to walk as Jesus walked, to pursue the prophets' vision of a just society, and to refuse to profit from that which brings harm to strangers across the globe might all seem similarly foolish at times. Faith, however, kept looking up and ahead for the coming rains. Faith still looks to the clouds and persists in living now so as to have no regrets on that day when Christ comes to judge the earth.

A third thread running throughout this chapter is that *faith invests in eternal goods*. The most fully developed examples of faith in Hebrews 11 are the examples of Abraham and Moses (11:8-20, 23-29). Both left behind a higher status and embraced a lower one— Abraham and his family by leaving their native land to become rootless aliens in a foreign land, Moses by leaving Pharaoh's household—in order to gain the greater promises of God. Neither Abraham nor Moses counted this a loss, however, because they knew God and God's promises to be real. Because of their faithful obedience, God's purposes in this world were achieved.

Many people have lived out a similar pattern. Readers may be familiar with the stories of Antony of the desert or Francis of Assisi. Both were born to prosperous families and had promising futures as the world has tended to gauge success. Both, however, heard the call of God and had their ambitions awakened to something greater than their influential families and considerable wealth could provide. Leaving home, family, and the future that was theirs by birth, they set out to follow God and labor for the eternal rewards of enjoying God's company forever, the rewards of the "new birth" in Christ.

This transformation can take many different forms. For one couple, it took the shape of deciding to live well below their means, purchasing a home that was much smaller than they could have afforded, and driving cars that were functional rather than flashy, so that they would have significant resources available to invest in people and getting the lives of others on more secure footing. No longer valuing or pursuing what many of their neighbors and associates considered highly desirable was risky. They opened themselves up to being thought foolish or odd. They accepted, however, that this world was not their lasting home and that real priority needed to be given to responding faithfully to God's call, to serving God's purposes, and, thus, to serving other people.

A fourth thread is that *faith acts in the confident hope of the Resurrection*. God will make life spring forth again where there is no life, just as surely as God made the visible creation where there was no visible material (11:3). God's power to supply life where none exists is seen in the birth of Isaac (and through Isaac, a countless multitude) to an elderly couple whose reproductive capacities had long since "died" (11:11-12). This thread emerges in the tapestry of the chapter again as the author recounts the most dramatic test of Abraham's obedience (11:17-19). What could have made Abraham willing to follow through when God told him to offer Isaac as a burnt offering? Genesis does not tell us what was going through Abraham's mind, but the preacher has an answer. Since God's promises were completely reliable, Abraham must have reasoned, God would bring Isaac back to life from the dead so the promise of descendants "through Isaac" would still be fulfilled.

Near the end of the preacher's list of examples, he speaks of "women" who "received their dead through resurrection" along with "others" who "were tortured, not accepting release, so that they might obtain a better resurrection" (11:35). The author no doubt has in mind women like the widow of Zarephath and the Shunammite woman, whose deceased sons Elijah and Elisha restored to them (1 Kings 17:17-24; 2 Kings 4:18-37). But these sons, like the people whom Jesus himself restored from death to the life of the body during his earthly ministry, would die again. The writer of Hebrews contrasts them with those who died in the hope of a "better resurrection," namely resurrection to eternal life. The preacher almost certainly has in mind here certain Jewish men and women who allowed themselves to be tortured to death during a horrific persecution under Antiochus IV around 166–165 BCE rather than renounce their faithfulness to the covenant (see 2 Maccabees 6:18-7:42). These martyrs could have been released from their torments at any time if they agreed to eat a mouthful of pork as a token of their willingness to set their ancestral law behind them. Instead, they persevered in faithfulness to God in the hope that God would raise them from the dead to live forever (2 Maccabees 7:9, 11, 14, 23, 29).

People of faith are not intimidated by human opposition (see Hebrews 11:23, 36-38) but act as reliable friends and servants of God. They prefer to endure temporary hardship and loss rather than break faith with God and lose eternal blessings in the world to come. Because they are confident that God gives life to the dead and that nothing can prevent God's promises from coming to pass, their integrity is not under the power of the government that threatens execution or the mob that threatens lynching or other physical harm (a faith exhibited daily by our sisters and brothers around the world). They can remain loyal to the God who has loved them and called them, rather than "shrink back"—the real opposite of faith (10:39)—in the face of temporal losses, however great.

A final thread is that *living by faith brings lasting honor*. Walking by faith leads to approval, both by God and by the people of God who continue to remember and celebrate those who exhibit faith (11:2, 4, 39). Had Abraham stayed in Haran and continued to flourish as a sheikh there, only the most specialized historians in Ancient Near Eastern Studies would know his name (if he happened to leave it behind on a clay seal or some such artifact). Had Moses supported the Pharaoh and his successors in the continued exploitation of the Hebrews, he would be at most a footnote in *The Cambridge Ancient History*. No one would have heard of the Christian saints Antony and Francis had they remained rich and comfortable members of the gentry. They might have been well-known and honored in their time and place but would soon have been forgotten thereafter. Their radical response to God's call, however, made them exemplars of the spiritual life, admired and imitated for centuries.

The first hearers, who were being stripped of their honor in their neighbors' eyes, would have found this powerful encouragement. It remains such to the many Christians throughout the world who still must make the choice to embrace "reproach for the Messiah" and leave behind "the treasures of Egypt" (11:25-26). Freedom from attachment to the rewards the society around us has the power to dispense or withhold is a necessary prerequisite to displaying the boldness in witness and in Christian practice that gratitude demands—and not just for Christians in overtly hostile environments.

The preacher challenges all Christians to decide for whose approval they will live. If we look for God's approval in everything we do, asking what will lead God to say, "Well done," we will enjoy the peace of single-mindedness and integrity of life. When faced with a decision, which choice would God applaud? When faced with temptation, what will lead to God's affirmation rather than self-condemnation? When reviewing our choice of career, our living and spending habits, our use of time—where does God affirm us, and where have we been living to please ourselves or to find affirmation by living up to the standards promoted by media?

The preacher implicitly criticizes those who exhibit too great a fascination with people whose greatest claim to fame is their glamour, notoriety, or wealth. Several decades ago, there was a popular show called *Lifestyles of the Rich and Famous*. It allowed viewers to "tour" palatial mansions, peer into the private lives of celebrated people, and hear about what the narrator lauded as "the good life." Such people really seemed to have made something of their lives, and many viewers no doubt admired them and wished to emulate them and enjoy the same "success." But the crucified Savior, into whose likeness Christians hope to grow, would never have been featured on that prime-time show, and the values the show represented would never serve to motivate faithful discipleship. A popular perversion of the gospel has grown up in Western culture suggesting that faith in God is a means to the very ends promoted in such a show. This is often called the "prosperity gospel," which promotes God as an endless supply of resources into which one may tap for material gain and the pleasures it offers. It is, sadly, not merely rampant in the West but has become one of our largest religious exports to developing nations.

The preacher draws our attention instead to the "Lifestyles of the Rich toward God," those who made a name for themselves not by achieving visible success, amassing fortunes, or climbing ladders of worldly power, but by following wherever God led and fearlessly pursuing the greater vision God implanted in their souls, even if this meant relinquishing all claims to status and place in this world. The most glamorous episode of *Lifestyles of the Rich and Famous* was but a pale shadow of the grand destiny appointed for those who heeded God's call, who were created for eternity and for communion with the invisible God.

Six

A Summons to Persevere in Gratitude

(Hebrews 12:1–13:25)

The preacher arrives at last at the exhortation that sums up the whole of his sermon: "Since we are receiving a kingdom that cannot be shaken, let us show gratitude!" (12:28). Gratitude moves us to endure for Jesus's sake what he endured for our sake. It impels us to move from the comfortable places and the embrace of our society into whatever spaces obedience to Jesus and loyalty to his global people lead us to enter. It causes us to value our adoption into God's family sufficiently to accept whatever cost is required on account of our association with that family. It summons us to discover ways to bear witness to God's gracious interventions in our lives and to offer the service God most desires—the investment of ourselves and our resources in our sisters and brothers in Christ throughout the world-wide communion, especially those who most need the embrace and support of their new family.

Grace is at the heart of the preacher's vision for the new life into which we have been invited as Christ's followers—indeed, as the "many sons and daughters" (2:10) that the firstborn has brought into God's household. This grace is not a one-way transaction, however. It is a dance that God has initiated first in creation, then afresh in the incarnation and death of the Son. And the preacher reminds those who have been invited that they must continue to move in step with the God who leads them, meeting grace (favor) with grace (gratitude) until they dance in the festal gathering of the angels and the righteous in eternity.

Persevering in the Right Race

People have always honored and celebrated great athletes, especially those who emerge as winners in games or events. This was no less true in the first century than it is today. On the way to victory, however, athletes have to endure rigorous training. If they are ever to attain the honor of winning, they must persevere in the face of the pain that accompanies training and competing and often also in the face of jeering crowds who prefer another athlete. Some events, like boxing, American football, or the ancient pancration (a no-holds-barred sparring event in Greek and Roman games), involve serious physical abuse. It is not surprising that members of minority groups like communities of Jews living outside of Israel and early Christians, who often had to endure insult and mistreatment, turned to athletic images to frame their experience positively, promoting pressing on in the face of hardship as the path to enjoying an honorable victory and depicting yielding to one's neighbors' pressures as being shamefully defeated by them.

The preacher used athletic imagery already in his sermon when he spoke of his audience's earlier experience of reproach, abuse, and imprisonment as "a great contest of sufferings" (10:32). Now he introduces the more specific images of the footrace (12:1-2) and the wrestling match (12:4) to help his hearers see themselves not as victims, but as potential victors if they but resist the urge to "throw in the towel."

> Since we indeed have so great a cloud of witnesses encircling us all about, and as we lay aside every weight and any sinful entanglement, let us continue to run the race laid out in front of us through perseverance, while we

> keep looking off toward the pioneer and perfecter of faith,
> namely Jesus, who, for the sake of the joy set in front of
> him, endured a cross, despising shame, and has sat down
> at God's right hand. Ponder him who endured such hos-
> tility from sinful people against himself so that you may
> not become fatigued, growing weary in your souls. While
> engaged in your wrestling match against sin, you have not
> yet resisted to the point of blood. (Hebrews 12:1-4)

From a purely practical point of view, withdrawing from the Christian group would seem like the path to recovering their formerly stable and secure lives and eventually even their good reputations among their neighbors. From the point of view of eternity, however, this is the path to defeat—to being deprived, by their own lack of fortitude, of the great honor and prize God holds out in front of them. The path to victory is none other than the path of continuing to live out their response of trust in and gratitude to God and God's Son in view of the gifts God has already lavished upon them and the future gifts God has promised.

The preacher urges his hearers to persevere in running "the race laid out before us" (12:1). This was the race they began running when they were baptized into Christ and taught the fundamental principles of the Christian faith (6:2-3). The finish line is none other than the threshold between life in the visible, material world and life in God's eternal realm—the threshold that Jesus fitted them to cross by virtue of his death and ascension (10:19-23). It is the finish line that Jesus had crossed ahead of them as their "forerunner" (6:19-20) and "pioneer" (2:10; 12:2). It is the race that had been run, and well run, by all the heroes of faith the preacher has just finished recalling for his hearers in chapter 11.

And these heroes now fill the stands of the cosmic stadium surrounding the believers. Those whose lives witnessed to the reality of God and God's promises now witness how *the Christian disciples* will run and whether *they* will also finish well. The believers have a choice as they leave the worship service in which they listen to this sermon being read to them. They can move about the streets of their city hyperaware of their non-Christian neighbors' opinions of them and perhaps even start living again in ways their neighbors will applaud as a welcome recovery. Or they can move about the streets of their city mindful that they stand in a cosmic stadium with Noah, Abraham, Moses, the Maccabean martyrs, and many others looking on from the invisible stands and perhaps continue to live in the ways *this* audience will applaud. Given the knowledge of God and of the truth of God's promises the members of this audience exhibited, they are in a far better position to judge the value and nobility of the believers' choices than the non-Christians who have themselves not yet "received knowledge of the truth" (10:26).

If the goal is no longer to recover our place in a society that is itself alienated from God but rather to continue to run in the direction of God's eternal realm, it becomes a priority to "lay aside every weight and any sinful entanglement" (12:1). The hearers have already laid many things aside. Their reputation in the eyes of their neighbors had become a "weight" that threatened to impede their progress in running toward the God who was calling them, and they had laid it aside, accepting that persevering in faith meant "being made a public spectacle through reproaches and mistreatment" (10:33). Some Christians had even tossed reputation aside, identifying with their disgraced sisters and brothers when they themselves had not been directly targeted (10:33-34). For some, their property had become a weight. They could have stopped running toward God and held onto it, but they laid it aside instead, "accepting the seizure of [their] goods with joy, knowing [themselves] to possess better and lasting property" (10:34). The preacher uses a stunning image for sin in 12:1, likening it to a close-fitting garment. Such attire might be fine for those who are sitting still or milling about, but for those whose minds are set on running and running well there is no place for a close-fitting outfit that restricts one's arm and leg movements, threatening to trip one up.

If one is to run the Christian life in a repressive environment, as with the first hearers of Hebrews and with our many sisters and brothers in certain Islamic, Hindu, and Communist nations, one must be willing to let go of everything that lies within one's neighbors' or the state's power to seize. As Martin Luther advised:

> If they would take your life,
> Goods, reputation, children, and wife,
> Let all these things go:
> They gain no victory thereby.
> The kingdom must remain ours![1]

The exhortation to "lay aside every weight" also challenges the Christian who faces little or no opposition from without. Even in the absence of such pressures, we bear weights that hinder our running the Christian race. We have the weight of parental expectations for the direction our lives will take, the weight of the standard of living our society nurtures us to seek, and the weight of our own dreams and ambitions for our lives in this world, as such dreams have been shaped apart from God's vision for us. And we are all faced with a wide range of potential "sinful entanglements" from the obvious indulgences pursued in defiance of God's commandments to ethically questionable decisions in pursuit of profit or advancement at work to the way we allow so many distracting entertainments to entangle us and keep us from running.

The preacher saves the crowning example of faith in action for this section. All of 11:1-40 built up to the exhortation and model found in 12:1-4. After directing our gaze toward those who watch and evaluate our running, the author directs our eyes to Jesus, who has run the course better and more completely than any other. Jesus is the pioneer of faith, running further ahead than anyone, having already entered heaven as our forerunner (6:19). Jesus is also the "perfecter of faith"—not "the perfecter of our faith," as in the King James Version or NRSV, but of "faith" itself, as in the NIV or CEB

(12:2).[2] He embodies faith more completely than any of the heroes celebrated thus far and has fully secured for all the faithful the heavenly goal they sought. Jesus exhibits faith much as did Abraham or Moses or the Maccabean martyrs: he sought God's ends and God's rewards no matter what hardship or shame that quest brought him on the limited stage of this life. The end of Jesus's story, namely, being given the highest honor possible in the cosmos, the place at the right hand of God, proves the wisdom of his choices. It also demonstrates that the way to eternal honor is the way of the cross, the way of giving one's life over to God's purposes rather than holding onto life for one's own gratification and fulfillment.

The racecourse that had been laid out for Jesus, through disgrace and hardship to honor, is also "the race laid out in front of" the preacher's first hearers. Indeed, Jesus ran the course first, according to the preacher, because God knew that his followers would have to run this particular course and, in this way, qualified Jesus to act as a sympathetic and competent mediator and help for his followers (2:10, 16-18). It remains the racecourse that many Christians *must* run today if they are to remain faithful. All Christians, however, have opportunities to train themselves in setting aside their neighbors' values and expectations—to set aside what their society has taught them makes a person honorable or gives worth—in favor of learning how to live in the often different ways and with the often different priorities and practices that God values and win the applause of heaven.

The preacher wants considering Jesus to have yet another effect on his hearers, however. Considering how much Jesus endured on their behalf—the humiliation, the pain, the laying aside of his own interests—should both embolden and shame them to endure as much for Jesus in return. If Jesus went "all in" to restore them to God's favor, do they not owe it to Jesus to go "all in" to arrive at the goal he opened up for them? John Chrysostom, a great preacher and theologian of the early fifth century, did not miss this writer's challenge:

What he means is this: You have not yet submitted to death; your loss has extended to money, to reputation, to being driven from place to place. Christ however shed His blood for you, while you have not shed blood on your own part. He contended for the Truth even unto death fighting for you; while you have not yet faced dangers that threaten your life.[3]

They might understandably have grown weary in their constant struggle, their wrestling against sin, which in their circumstances meant the constant temptation to return to the comfort, status, and security of the lives they left behind. But if they consider how much further Jesus went for them, how much more he endured for them, they might find their own strength rekindled. After all, they had "not yet resisted to the point of blood" (12:4) as the price of their loyalty to their great Benefactor, who allowed his own blood to be spilled in order to sanctify them (13:13). The preacher understood, and wanted his hearers to understand, that Jesus's death for them did more than transfer some gift to them. It bound the parties together in a life-debt, with those who have received Jesus's benefits bound to give back to Jesus as he gave to them. The apostle Paul understood this as well and stated it quite directly: Christ "died on behalf of all in order that those who continued living might live no longer for themselves, but for him who died and was raised on their behalf" (2 Corinthians 5:15). The measure of the giver's investment sets the measure of the beneficiary's gratitude.

In the Crucible of God's Classroom

The preacher goes even further in his attempt to change his audience's perception of the struggles and hardships they endure as a result of their perseverance in gratitude and loyal obedience to God. He suggests that the hardships themselves can be understood as a sign of God's favor. Because God has adopted the hearers as God's own sons and daughters, the difficulties that come their way as a result of their faithful response to God can be seen as the formative discipline that naturally falls to children growing up in a household (12:5-11). The difficulties they face prove their divine adoption (12:8). Further, they present the hearers with opportunities for growth in their character, refining their commitment to virtue in their relationship with God, exercising and strengthening their alignment with "righteousness," that is, with acting justly toward God, their great benefactor (12:10-11). The end result is "a share in God's holiness" (12:10), the "sanctification without which no one will see the Lord" (12:14). What their neighbors intended as a stigma that would make them give up their faith the author turns into a proof of their noble adoption into God's own family and a great impetus to persevere.

This strategy is a bit risky, and we need to be particularly careful in thinking about how these words of Hebrews continue to speak to us. First, the preacher is not speaking about any and every negative experience, whether disease, accident, or other tragedy. Rather, he speaks here very specifically about those negative experiences that his hearers have endured due to their neighbors' disapproval of their commitment to Christ and the changes in lifestyle they have observed as a result. The author also does not explain the losses and hardships the hearers have endured as punishment for past sins. The preacher introduces this paragraph with a quotation of Proverbs 3:11-12 (Hebrews 12:5-6), and that older text does indeed speak of corrective discipline, using phrases like "when you are punished by him" and "the Lord . . . chastises every child whom he accepts" (NRSV). But the preacher himself does not carry these elements of the quotation into his interpretation. He never suggests that the hearers have met with painful experiences because they did something wrong in God's sight and now have to suffer. He knows that the opposite has been the case (10:35-36). Rather, he recommends that they view these experiences entirely as training exercises God has placed in front of them to shape them. This is in keeping with popular philosophical conceptions of God testing, training, and shaping the wise person through hardships, making him or her worthy of God's company.[4] Embracing loss for the sake of remaining loyal and obedience to God is precisely the way that the Son himself "learned obedience," specifically "through what he suffered" (5:7-8). Why should the "many sons and daughters" (2:10) not learn obedience by the same path?

The primary danger facing the preacher's audience was succumbing at last to their neighbors' attempts to shame them. He wants them to consider a very different dynamic at work: they are not ultimately being *shamed*, but rather being *shaped* by their steadfast endurance in the face of this negative pressure. They are being shaped, moreover, for a glorious future in God's eternal kingdom. The hurtful behaviors themselves are still inflicted by "sinful people" (as they were upon Jesus himself, 12:3), and these "sinful people" do not inflict this suffering on God's behalf or with God's authorization. Nevertheless, the Christians can encounter difficulties considering how God will use these experiences to train them for more lasting, good results. As with the mental frame of the contest and the race, the image of divine training also provides the opportunity for the beleaguered Christians to regard themselves no longer as passive victims but as active agents digging in their heels in a wrestling match with sin or embracing hardship for the opportunity it gives to strengthen their moral fiber and refine their single-hearted commitment to God and the destiny God has offered them.

The preacher speaks, once again, very directly to Christians in repressive nations, urging them to value the experiences that test their faith and commitment, giving them the unwelcome yet wholesome opportunity to grow in their courageous witness and loyalty to God. His interpretation of difficulty as formative discipline, however, offers encouragement to Christians in all settings. Whenever the path of fidelity to God means facing human opposition, giving up something pleasurable, or denying ourselves in some way to advance God's purposes or another person's well-being, we are invited to embrace that path as an experience that will bring us into deeper solidarity with Jesus the Son. At every such juncture, we have the opportunity to learn obedience to God's will in a deeper way or to work against God's formation of our souls and character.

Running Well Together

The preacher returns to a theme that has run throughout his sermon: our mutual responsibility to assist one another to persevere in loyalty toward God and God's Son and to continue to choose courses of action that honor them and their gifts.

> Keep pursuing peace with all people and holiness, without which no one will see the Lord, keeping an eye out lest anyone fall short of God's gift, lest any root of bitterness spring up through which many become defiled, lest there be any fornicator or worldly minded person like Esau was—who for a single meal sold his rights as the firstborn. For you know that afterwards, when he wanted to inherit the blessing, he was rejected as unfit, for he found no place for repentance, even though he sought it with tears.
>
> (Hebrews 12:14-17)

The preacher commissions everyone in the group to "keep an eye out" for signs that a brother or sister in the family of faith is faltering, in need of encouragement, or in need of someone who will intervene and help him or her make faithful and wise decisions.

To "fall short of God's gift"—to withdraw from the Christian group rather than press on to the threshold of their eternal inheritance (compare 4:1)—is a real danger among his audience. Some have already begun that process of withdrawing (10:25), seeking peace with their neighbors and the enjoyment again of a quiet and stable life free from the harassment that association with Christ and withdrawal from the religious practices of their neighbors had brought. The preacher believes such wavering Christians to be walking in the footsteps of Esau (Genesis 25:29-34). Coming home famished from the field, Esau found Jacob preparing a pot of stewed lentils. When Esau told his brother to dish some out for him, Jacob demanded Esau first give him his birthright, the right of the firstborn to a larger share of their parents' estate. Esau's desire to assuage the temporary cravings and discomfort of hunger led him to make a remarkably short-sighted decision, with the result that the line of God's promise would be traced from Abraham and Isaac through Jacob rather than Esau. The comment by the narrator in Genesis is significant: "Thus Esau despised his birthright" (Genesis 25:34 NRSV). The preacher likens the choice that some Christians have taken (and that others in his audience are perhaps contemplating) to Esau's choice in order to drive home the foolishness of jeopardizing eternal benefits for temporary pleasure. This is the opposite of what Moses (Hebrews 11:24-26) and Jesus (12:2) did, preferring temporary hardship for the sake of gaining or retaining eternal benefits.

The preacher uses Esau's story to achieve a second effect, reinforcing the danger of making such a foolish choice that shows contempt for God's gifts and God's friendship by throwing them aside lightly. The preacher has read two different events in the Genesis narrative as though they stood in a cause-and-effect relationship. In Genesis, however, Esau himself clearly understood his rights as a firstborn and his father's blessing to have been two separate things, even though Jacob had managed to deprive him of each on respective occasions. The first was earlier in their lives; the second occurred as Isaac lay on his deathbed, with Rebekah helping Jacob to pass himself off to his father as Esau so as to receive not only the larger share of the inheritance due the firstborn, but also the blessing due the firstborn (Genesis 27:1-40). The preacher focuses, however, on Esau's lamenting to his father, Isaac, after Isaac has blessed Jacob. But the deed, once done, cannot be undone, and Esau is left in great distress for what he has lost. In the same way, those in the preacher's congregation who choose to disregard and lay aside God's gifts might not find an opportunity to reverse the decision later.

All can agree that Esau provides a stellar example of a person who made foolish choices, trading away the advantages that were his by birth and that would have come to him in the future for a short-lived bit of gratification in the present. Are we as clear-sighted when it comes to our own decisions and the priorities they reflect? Even if we were to enjoy the possession of the whole world but not be rich toward God, we would still be found fools when we stand at the threshold of eternity (Mark 8:36-38). But how many of us are in danger of being found fools and selling our eternal inheritance for a whole lot less than the world? Perhaps it is for a moment of compromise at work; perhaps it is for an extramarital affair; perhaps it is for many small, self-serving choices.

Standing at the threshold of the unshakable kingdom into which Christ stands prepared to welcome us, how will we respond to God? How will we keep our ambitions trained and our hearts fixed on the lasting goods before us, rather than being distracted by temporal ambitions? We need to be watchful over our own hearts and minds, to be sure, fearing those suggestions and desires that will lead us into places of disobedience and of dishonoring the Lord who has redeemed us. The way back may not be so clear and easy (12:17). But, the preacher reminds us, we need to be watchful over one another as well. When a sister loses sight of why certain pleasures need to be denied or certain difficult circumstances embraced rather than fled, we are called to help raise her eyes back to Jesus. When a brother is wearied by a long struggle against the hostility of unbelievers or the tenacity of his own flesh, we are called to "straighten the drooping arms and weak knees" and help him keep running toward God (12:12). If we love, support, and invest ourselves in one another now as sisters and brothers, we will not fail to attain our inheritance as the many sons and daughters.

A Final Warning to Respond Well

As the preacher moves toward the close of his sermon, it is natural, even standard practice, for him to begin to gather up some of the principal themes and their practical implications he has been exploring. The principal theme has been God's unprecedented generosity toward those who have aligned themselves with God's Son and the unprecedented advantages these people now enjoy. We should not be surprised, then, to find a significant amount of "review" of that theme in these closing paragraphs.

By way of review, the preacher presents two striking vignettes of how people have found themselves standing before God, encountering God in their midst (12:18-24). The first presents a fearsome scene: the appearance of God at Mount Sinai in the midst of "burning fire and darkness and gloom and stormy winds and the blast of a trumpet and the rumbling of words" (12:18-19; see Exodus 19:12-19; Deuteronomy 4:11-12; 5:22-23). The preacher combines many details from the Old Testament accounts of this scene, including the command that not even an animal was permitted to touch the mountain and, if it did, it was to be stoned to death (Hebrews 12:20; Deuteronomy 9:19). He recalls thus the restrictions on access to God under the old covenant and the strictness of their enforcement (see Hebrews 9:1-10). The overall mood was one of abject fear (such that even Moses trembled!) that could not be endured for long.

The second vignette, by stark contrast, displays a scene of celebration and joyful worship, with "myriads of angels in festive praise" and "the spirits of the righteous that have been brought to their destination" (Hebrews 12:22-23). This destination is the heavenly Jerusalem, the promised city of God and homeland for the people of faith (12:22). This is the confident approach to God that Jesus has made possible for the hearers (see 9:11–10:22), and the preacher is not reticent to remind them once again of the cost Jesus shouldered to bring them this gift: "the blood of sprinkling that speaks a better word than the blood of Abel" (12:24), the blood that removes the memory and defilement of sin rather than calls out for justice against sin (Genesis 4:10).

The recollection of God's appearance at Mount Sinai to give the Law through Moses provides the opportunity for a final warning not to neglect what God has spoken "in a Son" (1:2), the "great deliverance" that Jesus and his apostles had announced and God had attested (2:2-4). If the people of Israel could not escape the consequences of failing to heed "the one who admonished them on earth" (12:25), then surely the people who have received God's great promises in Jesus will not escape the consequences of ignoring the admonition that has come to them from heaven. While the preacher's warning here recalls very similar ones given earlier in his sermon (see especially 2:1-4; 10:26-31), he develops it in a different way. The admonition to which he refers speaks about the calamity that will befall creation at the end of this age, an event from which deliverance or salvation remains necessary and sure to come. Referring to the tradition that an earthquake accompanied the voice of God at Sinai (as in Judges 5:4-5 and Psalm 68:7-8), he writes:

> His voice shook the earth at that time, but now he promises, saying: "Yet one more time I will shake not only the earth but also the heaven." By saying "yet one more time," he signals the removal of the things that can be shaken . . . in order that the things that cannot be shaken may remain.
> (Hebrews 12:26-27)

Like other New Testament authors (notably those of 2 Peter 3:10; Revelation 21:1), the preacher believes that the present created order will cease to exist. Unlike the author of Revelation, he does not look forward to "a new heaven and a new earth" (Revelation 21:1), but only to the disclosure of the eternal realm of God's dwelling, currently invisible and inaccessible because the material creation stands in the way—just as the first chamber of the sanctuary stood in the way of and obscured sight of and access to the Holy of Holies (9:8-9). In light of these expectations, it is important indeed to have and keep the connections that grant one access to God's eternal realm, lest one cease to exist along with the material creation. The preacher's expectations also reinforce the relative value he has assigned to everything that could be possessed or enjoyed in the life of *this* world vis-à-vis what will be possessed and enjoyed *forever* in the life of the coming world (2:5).

Repeating a pattern he has established throughout the sermon, the preacher turns again from warning to more positive exhortation, specifically framed once more to motivate his hearers to hold onto their grace relationship with God through God's Son:

> Therefore, since we are receiving a kingdom that cannot be shaken, let us hold fast to gratitude, by means of which let us serve God in a well-pleasing manner with reverent awe—for our God is a consuming fire!
>
> (Hebrews 12:28-29)

The fact that God is extending significant favor toward the hearers (here, entrance into the "unshakable kingdom" of God's eternal presence) is the cause that must result in a reciprocal effect: since we are receiving this gift, "therefore . . . let us" respond appropriately, that is, gratefully. We have observed the same logic and, indeed, the same phrasing at other major junctures in the preacher's sermon (4:14-16; 10:19-25).

Both the amplitude of the benefactor's honor and the magnitude of the favors he or she confers have bearing on the scale of the gratitude that constitutes an appropriate response. In this particular instance, the scope of God's favor shown particularly in the self-giving of God's Son calls forth a totalizing response of gratitude on the part of those whom the Son has made part of his family. Isaac Watts captured this with exquisite clarity in his hymn "When I Survey the Wondrous Cross":

Were the whole realm of Nature mine,
That were a present far too small;
Love so amazing, so divine,
Demands my soul, my life, my all.

The preacher's hearers had given a great deal in commitment to their heavenly patron. Some had decided that they had given too much, that the cost of their connection outweighed the benefits. The sermon "to the Hebrews" has been all about correcting such accounting. What God's Son has secured for human beings is infinite in value, even as, for the Son, it was infinite in cost, for it required all from him. Our connection and our ongoing relationship with such a savior, correspondingly, are worth our all as well.

The question the sermon raises for us is not, "Am I doing enough to be sure of my salvation?" This question is misguided, because it is never a question of our earning such a reward. But the preacher does want to raise the question and leave the question ever ringing in our minds, "Am I giving back to Jesus, and to the God in whose favor Jesus has allowed me to stand, the honor, the loyalty, and the service that their favor toward me merits?" And if we correctly evaluate the merit, we will know that we can never return "enough" short of giving "all." It is by this path, however, that we arrive at discovering how to "serve God in a well-pleasing manner with reverent awe" (12:28), as we draw more and more of ourselves and of all we involve ourselves in toward an intentional response of gratitude to God and his Christ.

The preacher will not allow us to forget the side of God we so often wish to ignore or to deny. He urges his hearers to persevere in a life shaped by gratitude toward God, "because our God is a consuming fire" (12:29). He is quoting here from Deuteronomy, where these very words are used to motivate obedience to the old covenant and, particularly, the complete avoidance of idolatry (Deuteronomy 4:24). Once more the preacher will not allow Christians to divorce the God of the Old Testament from the God of the New Testament. The nature of the covenant has changed dramatically, as the preacher celebrated at length (Hebrews 8:1–10:18); the people's access to God has changed dramatically; but God's character remains constant. God remains "the rewarder of those who earnestly seek him" (11:6) and the one who upholds his holiness and honor against those who "trample the Son of God underfoot . . . and meet the Spirit of grace with outrageous insult" (10:29).

Showing Gratitude

The specific instructions of chapter 13 seamlessly extend the exhortation begun at the end of chapter 12 as the preacher suggests a number of agenda items that fill out what "showing gratitude" (12:28) looks like in everyday actions and orientations. He gives some verbal cues concerning the connectedness of all this material:

"... let us keep serving in a manner *well-pleasing* to God."
(12:28)

"... with such sacrifices God is *well-pleased*." (13:16)

"... working in us what is *well-pleasing* in his sight."
(13:21)

The staccato instructions of 13:1-6 (and beyond) fall like bullet points under the principal exhortation to show gratitude, fleshing out the picture of the kind of response to grace that will please the divine Giver, all the while acknowledging that it is God who is at work within us to move us to become well-pleasing in the sight of him who remains "the judge of all" (12:23). God's *grace* achieves its goals in us and for us by provoking the response of *gratitude* that transforms the orientation and direction of our lives.

The first cluster of instructions directs the hearers to those affections and practices that will keep the Christian group and the commitment of each individual disciple strong, particularly in the midst of a hostile environment:

> Let mutual love continue. Do not neglect to show hospi-
> tality to strangers, for by doing that some have entertained
> angels without knowing it. Remember those who are in
> prison, as though you were in prison with them; those who
> are being tortured, as though you yourselves were being
> tortured. (13:1-3 NRSV)

In its laudable effort to provide a gender-inclusive translation, the NRSV loses some of the flavor of the preacher's first instruction, which specifically urges that the believers continue to live out the ideal of *philadelphia*—the love that characterizes siblings—among their fellowship; a better translation is, "Keep loving one another with the love of sisters and brothers" (13:1).[5] This was a rather well-articulated ideal in the Greco-Roman world. The relationship between siblings was to be one of trust, solidarity, and cooperation, never competition. Siblings were to treat their possessions as common property, sharing as any had need, and they were to pursue harmony, seek to include each other in the advantages each enjoyed, and protect each other's reputation. Indeed, there is a great deal of overlap between the ethic promoted between natural siblings and the specific instructions we find Jesus and the apostles giving to the early Christian communities.[6]

The practice of opening up their homes to one another (13:2) was an important manifestation of the larger family that communal trust in Jesus and adoption into God's household created. Without a strong commitment to hospitality, the Christians would have nowhere to gather, and the movement of traveling missionaries, teachers, and emissaries would have been significantly hindered. Such continues to be the way Christians operate in many countries where public gathering in the name of Jesus is illegal. Even where we enjoy dedicated church buildings, however, there is a great deal to be gained when Christians open up their homes to smaller groups for prayer, study, mutual encouragement, and the planning of service and outreach. And in a time when many Christians must become refugees to save their own and their families' lives, what a gift from God it would be and what an affirmation of the truth that they have been united to a larger family for them to find the doors of other Christians' homes open to them.

In the first century, it was particularly important that believers who were most marginalized, most cut off from their natural networks of support, and most subjected to hardship should experience this level of love and commitment from their fellow Christians. Those Christians who were not in prison were to mobilize relief and encouragement for their sisters and brothers who were in prison "as though you were fellow prisoners together" and for those who were suffering physical mistreatment, a common enough side effect of the ancient prison and judicial system, "as though you were the one living in their body" (13:3). Crossing the battle line to show solidarity with such people was risky, and it remains risky now, but the loyalty we owe our divine Benefactor includes showing fidelity to the at-risk members of God's household. Jesus himself made this amply clear in his vision of the last judgment: "to the extent that you did these things for the humblest of my sisters and brothers, you did it for me" (Matthew 25:40). Does our level of personal investment in the faith and the fate of our Christian sisters and brothers suffering such marginalization throughout the world this very day match the personal investment we would make were members of our natural families facing such dire circumstances? To the extent that it does, their experience of the family of God—and our experience of the family of God—becomes real.

It is probably appropriate that instructions regarding nurturing positive and committed attachments among the Christian family be accompanied by instructions concerning necessary detachments. Attachment to property or any desire to recover their former financial standing (see 10:34) would have led the preacher's hearers to slink away and find their way back into their former social networks, so the preacher urges them to be content with what they *do* have. They have nothing less than the promise of God never to abandon them, which ought to, in turn, allow them to have the utmost confidence in the face of their human opponents (13:5-6)! The audience may well have recalled the preacher's encouragements to them to continue to show "boldness" owning their connection to Christ and to his family, with the result that they will remain on track to receiving the eternal gifts prepared for them in the future (10:35-36).

While the implications of such admonitions for Christians in repressive environments are once again clear, their implications for Western Christians are equally clear. "Contentment" is not a core value in capitalist economies. Quite the opposite: it is the lack of contentment that energizes economies by stimulating both the amassing and the spending of capital. The preacher joins other New Testament voices advising against "building bigger barns" (see Luke 12:15-21) or "spending what you get on gratifying your-selves" (James 4:3), urging instead that we learn to define "enough" with sufficient modesty to release capital to invest in supplying the needs of God's marginalized sons and daughters. It is perhaps in connection with this holy value of contentment that the preacher warns against extramarital affairs, which break down the relation-ships most closely intended to support one another's perseverance in godliness (13:4).

Each generation of disciples can continue to maintain the same trust they have observed in the leading figures of previous genera-tions of Christ's saints because "Jesus Christ is the same yesterday, today, and to the extent of the age" (13:7-8). We can trust him not to change—not to be willing to help his followers today but not tomorrow or not to have made promises that he will not keep. His firmness and constancy are ever an aid to our own. At the same time, his loyalty *to* those he came to help requires loyalty to match *in* those he came to help.

> Therefore Jesus—in order that he might sanctify the peo-
> ple through his own blood—also suffered outside the gate.
> Let us accordingly continue to go out to him "outside

the camp," bearing his reproach, for here we don't have a lasting city, but we are looking for the one that is coming.

(13:12-14)

The preacher recalls very specifically Jesus's crucifixion outside of the city gates of Jerusalem, the obedience unto death that Jesus offered and the depth of humiliation he endured (12:2), for the sake of others, including those gathered to hear this sermon. Gratitude for "love so amazing, so divine," as expressed in the hymn, requires remaining loyal to such a benefactor, especially when loyalty is costly.

Seneca, the first-century philosopher and statesman, wrote concerning the cost of gratitude, "It is the ungrateful person who thinks: 'I should have liked to return gratitude, but I fear the expense, I fear the danger, I shrink from giving offense; I would rather consult my own interest.'"[7] The preacher has urged his hearers from the beginning to the end of his sermon not to be that person. What Jesus bore for my sake, to extend favor to me, I must be willing to bear for his sake, to preserve the grace relationship into which he invited me. For the preacher's congregation, this very directly meant being willing to be shamed by their neighbors on account of their attachment and loyalty to Jesus (Hebrews 10:32-34; 13:3). It meant continuing to live in their city as people who were no longer at home in it, no longer a part of its networks and structures. They had "gone outside the camp" of their neighbors just as Jesus had gone "outside the gates" for them, and they had to commit to continuing on that same trajectory. But the preacher assures them one last time that the path "outside the camp" of the city, which is not their true and lasting home, is the path that leads to the city of the living God, which is their eternal home in the unshakable realm (13:14).

Once again, we must allow ourselves to be struck by the directness with which the first-century preacher speaks to twenty-first-century Christians in nations that are hostile to the Christian presence in their midst. But our response cannot be one of relief that it speaks thus to Christians other than ourselves, not least because the preacher has already pushed us to seek out avenues of solidarity and support in regard to them. We are equally called to "go out" from the structures and expectations our society has erected around us and move more and more fully into a new space outside of that camp. As we move more fully into the economy that Jesus and his apostles sought to shape among the Christ-followers, we move out from the standard practices and procedures of the worldly economy. As we move more fully into solidarity with the family of God drawn from every nation, language, people, and tribe, we move out from the nationalism (and even tribalism) that characterizes worldly politics. Do we not move out as far as our Lord calls us to move—do we not offer him the service that gratitude demands—because we fear the reproach or the expense?

The psalmist once asked, "What shall I give to the Lord in return for all the benefits I have received from him?" (Psalm 116:12). His response consisted of a litany of liturgical acts that bore public witness to God's gifts and expressed the psalmist's deep thanks. In similarly liturgical terms, the preacher calls his hearers to bring to God the sacrifices that are God's due:

> Through Jesus Christ, let us continue always to offer up to God the sacrifice of praise—that is, the fruit of lips professing his name. Let us not neglect doing good and sharing, for God is well pleased with sacrifices of this kind.
>
> (Hebrews 13:15-16)

When Greek and Roman ethicists outlined what it meant to receive a gift and show gratitude well, it always involved bearing verbal and public testimony to a giver's generosity and to one's thankfulness for specific and helpful gifts and interventions. It was not just saying "thank you" to the giver, but bearing witness generously to third parties. This contributed significantly to the giver's honor in the community and was within the power of any recipient of his or her favors to do. Such testimony would indeed be a "sacrifice" for the preacher's audience, since the quieter they were about their connection with Jesus, the better things would go for them, but such was the "thank offering" that Jesus, their mediator, and God, their heavenly benefactor, merited. It was only by such testimony that their neighbors would ever consider joining themselves to a God who was truly present with God's people. The growth of the church in the third century, when hostility was at its peak and the martyrs' loyalty and testimony to their Patron at its boldest and most costly, shows the preacher's instincts to have been correct. Taking stock of the ways in which God has intervened in one's life and being sufficiently bold to speak to others about what God has done and how thankful one is remain the cornerstone of evangelism and invitation for Christians in any setting.

The preacher also highlights once again the value of "doing good and sharing" as the other principal component of their service, the sacrifices due God in grateful response to God's favor. He himself no doubt has primarily in mind "doing good and sharing" with the more marginalized members of the household of faith (see 6:9-10). In their situation this, too, was a personal sacrifice, since openly identifying with those whom the society sought to shame and reform—assisting them to resist being reformed!—would draw society's negative attention to them as well. It is to this level of mutual commitment, however, that the preacher has consistently called all of his hearers, speaking quite clearly across the centuries to us as well. The value of "doing good and sharing" in God's sight as an expression of our gratitude also provides the foundation for all that we might do to reach out beyond the household of faith and joins these acts of service with our profession of gratitude to God. We can give both God and our neighbor the gift of hearing, "We give because God gave."

The underlying message of the Letter to the Hebrews is ultimately one of grace. It is not, however, about grace merely as something that benefits us, but about grace as something that, having benefited us, shapes the whole of our lives into a consistent walk and witness of gratitude to God and to the Savior who reconnected us with God. The preacher focuses our hearts and minds on the magnitude of the favors we have received and are yet to receive from God so that we might fathom and feel more and more fully the magnitude of the gratitude that is God's due and give ourselves just as fully to God and God's cause in our world. It is a call to remain in grace by persevering in gratitude. It is no mere formality, then, when he concludes his sermon with the prayer, "May grace continue to be with you all" (13:25).

For Further Study

Cockerill, Gareth. *The Epistle to the Hebrews*. New International Commentary on the New Testament. Grand Rapids, MI: Eerdmans, 2012.

Craddock, F. B. "Hebrews," in vol. 12 of *The New Interpreter's Bible*, edited by Leander Keck, 1–174. Nashville: Abingdon, 1998.

deSilva, David A. *The Letter to the Hebrews in Social-Scientific Perspective*. Cascade Companions. Eugene, OR: Cascade, 2012.

deSilva, David A. *Perseverance in Gratitude: A Socio-Rhetorical Commentary on the Epistle to the Hebrews*. Grand Rapids, MI: Eerdmans, 2000.

Guthrie, George H. *Hebrews*. New International Version Application Commentary. Grand Rapids, MI: Zondervan, 1998.

Johnson, Luke T. *Hebrews: A Commentary*. New Testament Library. Louisville: Westminster John Knox, 2006.

Koester, Craig. *The Epistle to the Hebrews*. The Anchor Yale Bible Commentaries. Garden City, NY: Doubleday, 2001.

Nelson, Richard D. *Raising Up a Faithful Priest: Community and Priesthood in a Biblical Theology*. Louisville: Westminster/John Knox Press, 1993.

Pfitzner, Victor C. *Hebrews*. Abingdon New Testament Commentaries. Nashville: Abingdon Press, 1997.

Thompson, James W. *Hebrews*. Paideia: Commentaries on the New Testament. Grand Rapids, MI: Baker Academic, 2008.

Witherington, Ben. *Letters and Homilies for Jewish Christians: A Socio-Rhetorical Commentary on Hebrews, James and Jude*. Downers Grove, IL: InterVarsity, 2007.

Notes

Introduction

1. *The Book of Common Prayer* (New York: Oxford University Press, 2007), 101.

1. The Sermon's Setting and the Son's Glory (Hebrews 1:1–2:4)

1. A powerful antidote to the attitude toward the Old Testament reflected here can be found in Brent A. Strawn, *The Old Testament Is Dying: A Diagnosis and Recommended Treatment* (Grand Rapids: Baker Academic, 2017). Pastors especially should take note of this resource.
2. William L. Lane, *Hebrews: A Call to Commitment* (Peabody, MA: Hendrickson, 1988), 15.
3. This reflects another connection with the Pauline mission, as Paul also remembers how his hearers' experience of the Holy Spirit's presence and power confirmed his message (see 1 Corinthians 2:1-5; Galatians 3:1-5).
4. Psalm 2:7, quoted in Hebrews 1:5a; Psalm 45:6-7, quoted in Hebrews 1:8-9; Psalm 110:1, quoted in Hebrews 1:13.
5. The word typically translated "world" in this verse does not refer to our everyday world. The preacher will make this plain in 2:5 when he says "It wasn't to angels that he subjected the coming world, concerning which we have been speaking," using the same Greek word for "world" as here. The "coming world" already exists—it is *God's* realm, which is only "coming" from the perspective of human beings, whose path into that world is temporarily blocked by the material earth and heavens (12:26-28).
6. Dio Chrysostom, *Oration* 74.21, 24.
7. See also Hebrews 8:1; 10:12; 12:2.
8. The author of Hebrews is not alone in speaking of salvation as something that lies ahead of the believer. See also Romans 13:11-14; Philippians 2:12-13; 3:10-15; 1 Peter 1:5, 9; 2:2.

2. Threshold Moments (Hebrews 2:5–4:13)

1. Jesus is remembered frequently to have referred to himself as "the Son of Man" (see Matthew 8:20; 9:6; 11:19; 12:8, 32, 40).

2. See, further, Ernst Becker, *The Denial of Death* (New York: Free Press, 1973), 11–24.

3. In its original context, Isaiah 8:17 spoke of the prophet's confident hope in God, but the preacher has carefully detached it from that context and set it as an independent statement within this new context. It seems highly likely that the audience would understand the "him" in whom Jesus places confidence to be the disciple. See David A. deSilva, *Perseverance in Gratitude: A Socio-Rhetorical Commentary on the Epistle "to the Hebrews"* (Grand Rapids: Eerdmans, 2000), 116–17.

4. Joseph M. Scriven, "What a Friend We Have in Jesus" (1855).

5. John Donne, Sermon XXXVII, preached upon Trinity Sunday, 1 Peter 1:17.

6. *The Book of Common Prayer* (New York: Oxford University Press, 2007), 167.

7. Aristotle, *Rhetoric* 2.28, my translation.

3. Responding Gracefully to Grace (Hebrews 4:14–6:20)

1. Borrowing a phrase from John Newton's hymn, "How Sweet the Name of Jesus Sounds."

2. This would—not incidentally—be in keeping with the two other uses of the word translated "although" in Hebrews (see 7:5; 12:17).

3. Seneca, *On Benefits* 3.1.1, Loeb Classical Library.

4. Dio Chrysostom, *Oration* 31.65, Loeb Classical Library.

5. For further information on the social context of "grace" in the Greco-Roman world and its import for reading the New Testament, see David A. deSilva, *Honor, Patronage, Kinship & Purity: Unlocking New Testament Culture* (Downers Grove, IL: InterVarsity, 2000), 95–156.

6. The use of agricultural images to articulate the relationship of benefactor and beneficiary—and the "natural" expectations that favor should beget favor—can be seen in literature as early as Isaiah's song of the vineyard (Isaiah 5:1-7). It is quite common in Seneca's *On Benefits*, a

priceless text for gaining an inside look at patronage, friendship, and reciprocity in the first century. One example: "The farmer will lose all that he has sown if he ends his labours with putting in the seed; it is only after much care that crops are brought to their yield; nothing that is not encouraged by constant cultivation from the first day to the last ever reaches the stage of fruit. In the case of benefits the same rule holds" (*Ben.* 2.11.4-5).

7. John Rippon, "How Firm a Foundation," *Selection of Hymns from the Best Authors, Intended to Be an Appendix to Dr. Watt's Psalms and Hymns* (New York: WIlliam Durell, 1792), 128.

4. A Full, Perfect, and Sufficient Sacrifice (Hebrews 7:1–10:18)

1. See, for example, *Testament of Levi* 3.4-8; Tobit 12:12, 15; Matthew 18:10; Revelation 8:3-4.

2. Pseudo-Philo, *Biblical Antiquities* 19.11. See also the testimony to Moses's powerful mediation in *Testament of Moses* 11.17.

3. This is probably the *historical* sense of Psalm 110:4 in its ancient Israelite context.

4. See, for another example, Wisdom of Solomon 9:8, where "Solomon" prays to God: "You said to build a temple on your holy mountain and an altar in the city of your dwelling, an imitation of the holy tent that you prepared beforehand from the beginning." References to a heavenly temple wherein God dwells can also be found in *2 Baruch* 4:1-7; Revelation 11:19; 15:5-8.

5. In the NRSV, for example, one can find words related to "perfection" in Hebrews 2:10; 5:9; 6:1; 7:11, 19, 28; 9:9, 11; 10:1, 14; 11:40; 12:2, 23. The CEB retains similar words in all these places save Hebrews 7:11; 10:14; and 12:2. The NRSV represents the family of Greek words built on the corresponding root quite well, though 5:14 and 11:40 should be added to the list.

6. See the classic expression of this in Wesley's sermon "Christian Perfection." See *John Wesley's Sermons*, ed. Albert C. Outler and Richard P. Heitzenrater (Nashville: Abingdon Press, 1991), 69–84.

7. See also the narratives of this event in Luke 24:44-53; Acts 1:1-11.

5. Faithful Response in Action (Hebrews 10:19–11:40)

1. Any notion of "figuring out *how*" is absent from the Greek. See, further, William L. Lane, *Hebrews 9-13*, Word Biblical Commentary 47b (Dallas: Word, 1991), 273, and Paul Ellingworth, *The Epistle to the Hebrews*, New International Greek Testament Commentary (Grand Rapids: Eerdmans, 1993), 526.

2. You can learn more both about the current plight of Christians in repressive countries and about opportunities to connect with them and support them through several well-vetted Christian outreaches, including Voice of the Martyrs (www.persecution.com), Open Doors (www.opendoorsusa.org), and Barnabas Aid (https://barnabasfund .org/us).

3. Paul was not at all ambiguous about the demand for transformation that God's grace placed upon us. See Galatians 5:16-25; 6:7-10; Romans 6:1-20; 8:2-14. These and many other texts are discussed in David A. deSilva, *Transformation: The Heart of Paul's Gospel* (Bellingham, WA: Lexham, 2014).

4. The cultivation of a heart and mind that are ever sensible of and attentive to God's presence and prompting is a major theme of spiritual classics like Brother Lawrence, *The Practice of the Presence of God*; Thomas à Kempis, *The Imitation of Christ*; and Jeremy Taylor, *The Rule and Exercises of Holy Living*.

6. A Summons to Persevere in Gratitude (Hebrews 12:1–13:25)

1. From Martin Luther, "Ein feste Burg is unser Gott" ("A Mighty Fortress Is Our God"), verse 4, author's translation.

2. See further the discussion in William L. Lane, *Hebrews 9-13*, Word Biblical Commentary 47b (Dallas: Word, 1991), 399 note k.

3. John Chrysostom, "Homily on Hebrews 12:4-10." Adapted from the translation by Frederic Gardiner from *Nicene and Post-Nicene Fathers*, First Series, Vol. 14, ed. Philip Schaff (Buffalo, NY: Christian Literature, 1889), 499.

4. The mid-first-century philosopher Seneca, for example, wrote a lengthy essay on this very theme ("On Providence," *De providentia*).

5. The CEB improves on the NRSV with "Keep loving each other like family."

6. See further David A. deSilva, *Honor, Patronage, Kinship & Purity: Unlocking New Testament Culture* (Downers Grove, IL: InterVarsity, 2000), 212–26.

7. Seneca, *On Benefits* 4.24.2; Loeb Classical Library.